BRITAIN IN OLD PHOTOGRAPHS

GLOUCESTERSHIRE COUNTY CRICKET CLUB

DEAN P. HAYES

SUTTON PUBLISHING LIMITED

Sutton Publishing Limited
Phoenix Mill · Thrupp · Stroud
Gloucestershire · GL5 2BU

First published 1998

British Library Cataloguing in Publication Data
A catalogue record for this book is available from the
British Library.

ISBN 0-7509-1909-4

Typeset in 10/12 Perpetua.
Typesetting and origination by
Sutton Publishing Limited.
Printed in Great Britain by
Ebenezer Baylis, Worcester.

This book is dedicated to Bert Avery, one of cricket's gentlemen.

1877 team. Back row, left to right: W.O. Mobberly, W. Fairbanks, G.F. Grace, F.G. Monkland, W.R. Gilbert, W.E. Midwinter. Front row: Capt H.B. Kingscote, F. Townsend, R.F. Miles, W.G. Grace (captain), E.M. Grace. After winning the Championship in 1876 Gloucestershire retained the title, winning eight of their nine matches and drawing the other. This summer marked the first appearance of W.E. Midwinter whom W.G. had met when touring Australia in 1873–4. He has a unique place in cricket history, for he was Gloucestershire's first full-time professional and is the only cricketer to play for both Australia and England in Test matches against each other. His first full appearance was in one of the most famous games in Gloucestershire's history, when they beat England at the Oval by 5 wickets.

CONTENTS

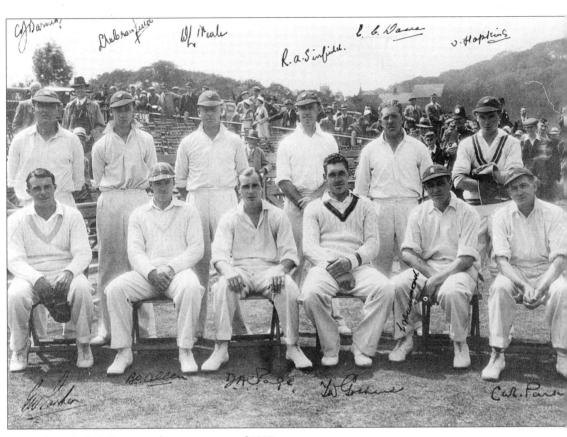

Autographed Gloucestershire team group of 1937.

INTRODUCTION

For 128 years now, Gloucestershire has flourished as a county cricket club; indeed the county of cricket's immortals, Dr W.G. Grace and Walter Hammond, of Jessop, Barnett and Graveney and (from the overseas treasure chest) of Procter, Zaheer and Walsh, epitomises for many the spirit of English cricket.

In 1870 Gloucestershire had a remarkable first season and the following spring the present county club was formed.

Gloucestershire's cricket roots go deep. In 1709 William Goldwin was appointed Master of Bristol Grammar School. Three years previously he had published a volume of Latin poems including '*In Certamen Pilae: Anglice a Cricket Match*'. This is the first printed reference of more than a line or two on the subject of cricket and it is possible therefore that Goldwin introduced the game into his school.

1729 gives us the first clear date for Gloucestershire's cricket history. The *Weekly Journal* for 20 September of that year reads as follows: 'Gloucester 15th September: On Monday the 22nd inst, will be played in the Town-Ham of this City, by 11 men of a side, a game at cricket for upwards of 20 guineas.' By 1752 we learn from Felix Farley's *Bristol Journal* that the game was being played in that city. In 1769 the *Gloucester Journal* reports a game at Cirencester, noting that 'some excellent matches have been lately played there for considerable sums'. Other early centres of the game were at Cheltenham, Clifton, Kingcote, Kingsdown and Minchinhampton.

The first noted player from Gloucestershire was H.R. Kingscote, who became President of MCC in 1827 at the age of twenty-four! One of his contemporaries was a Dr H.M. Grace who used to practise in the early morning on Durdham Downs, Bristol – the scene of the 1752 match. On marrying Martha Pocock of St Martin's Hill, Bristol, he settled at Downend in 1831. In due time Dr and Mrs Grace had five sons and four daughters – these formed a healthy nucleus for the club at Mangotsfield which he had formed in 1845! This later became the West Gloucestershire Club.

In 1854 Dr Grace played with his eldest son, Henry, and his brother-in-law, Alfred Pocock, for West Gloucestershire against the All England XI. The following year E.M Grace joined in. In 1858 the first representative county team, the Gentlemen of Gloucestershire, lost to I Zingari at Badminton. Four years later they played their first fixture against another county when they met Devonshire.

These developments paved the way for the formation on 3 November 1863 of the Cheltenham and County of Gloucester Cricket Club. This club was wound up on 14 March 1871 and the President, Lord Fitzhardinge, became a Vice-President of the new Gloucestershire County Cricket Club.

The most noteworthy occasion during these years probably took place in 1868 when E.M., W.G. and G.F. Grace all played in the Gloucestershire team which met for the first time against the MCC and Ground at Lord's. Between them they took 17 wickets and E.M. made the highest score. Not surprisingly, Gloucestershire won the match.

Dr Grace senior had subsequently got up several more or less casual county matches, but although he was always anxious to form a regular county club he didn't succeed in doing so until 1870. His untiring efforts resulted in Gloucestershire winning all five matches played that summer. The following spring the Gloucestershire County Cricket Club was formally founded.

During the 1871 season all the Grace brothers apart from Alfred played in the winning side against Surrey at the Oval. In 1873 the County Championship was inaugurated and Gloucestershire shared the title with Nottinghamshire. In both 1876

Tony Brown, Gloucestershire captain in 1973, talking to his team. Back row, left to right: J.H. Shackleton, J. Davey, D.A. Graveney, R.D.V. Knight, J.C. Foat, A.T. Brassington, G.G.M. Wiltshire (coach), R.B. Nicholls. Front row: R. Swetman, J.B. Mortimore, G.W. Parker (secretary), M.J. Procter, C.A. Milton, Sadiq Mohammed.

Gloucestershire team group, 1977. Back row, left to right: G.G.M. Wiltshire (coach), I.C. Crawford, J.H. Childs, J.H. Shackleton, B.M. Brain, A.S. Brown, A.J. Brassington, N.H.C. Cooper, J.C. Foat. Front row: D.A. Graveney, D.R. Shepherd, M.J. Procter, J. Davey, A.W. Stovold.

and 1877 the County won the championship without losing a match. In 1881 Gloucestershire were second, but were less successful after that, in spite of the fact that W. Midwinter had become, in 1877, the county's first regular professional, coming back from Australia to assist his native county. Between 1882 and 1894 Gloucestershire never had a season with more wins than losses. In 1891, 1893 and 1894 the county had the wooden spoon.

These latter years, however, saw the emergence of C.L. Townsend and G.L. Jessop. The advent of these two brilliant all-rounders seems to have stirred the Grand Old Man to even greater heights, for in 1895 W.G. Grace scored his famous thousand runs in May while in his forty-seventh year. This enormous achievement was largely instrumental in lifting Gloucestershire to fourth place in the championship. In 1896 they dropped to tenth and were skittled out for 17 by the visiting Australians. After the county had finished third in 1898, W.G. dropped a bombshell and announced his resignation from the captaincy. He severed his connections with the county, spending the rest of his life in the London area.

The new century saw a fresh captain in Gilbert Jessop, who stayed at the helm until 1912. He made over 2,000 runs and took over 100 wickets in 1900 as the county finished seventh. Thereafter Townsend could not play and the county's fortunes slumped. When the First World War intervened they were at the bottom of the table.

After the hostilities had ended several fine amateurs joined the Gloucestershire team, although the county was not so successful as it had been in the days of the Graces.

It is surprising that Gloucestershire's record was not better as this period saw the emergence of Walter Hammond and Tom Goddard. Hammond holds all the major Gloucestershire batting records: 2,860 runs in 1933; 33,664 runs for the county; thirteen centuries in 1938 and 113 hundreds in all county matches. Tom Goddard's off-break bowling reaped a rich harvest for many years. Gloucestershire's greatest achievement in the inter-war period was almost certainly the tied match against the 1930 Australians. The best years preceding the Second World War were 1936 and 1937, when the county was fourth, and 1939 when Hammond brought them to the third position.

Since the war Gloucestershire's fortunes have been mixed. The main weakness has usually been in the middle order batting, though an exception to this was Tom Graveney. He was an elegant craftsman who had every shot in the book. It was a severe blow to the county when, in 1960, he decided to move to Worcestershire after losing the captaincy to Tom Pugh. In the 1950s the county's batting was boosted by the dependable Crapp and the emerging talents of Arthur Milton.

In 1965 the county acquired the services of South African Mike Procter, a player who was to become arguably the world's greatest all-rounder. In 1968 Tony Brown, a cricketer with outstanding leadership qualities, was appointed captain and in 1973 he led the team to victory over Sussex in the Gillette Cup Final. Four years later Procter captained Gloucestershire to success in the Benson and Hedges Cup Final as they beat Kent by 64 runs.

At about this time Gloucestershire also had the services of two Pakistan Test players, Sadiq Mohammed and Zaheer Abbas, the latter having a brilliant season in 1976 when he scored 2,554 runs at an average of 75.11. There followed a few depressing seasons before, in 1986, under the leadership of David Graveney, the County finished runners-up in the Championship with West Indian import Courtney Walsh taking 118 wickets at a rate of 18.17 runs each.

Since Gloucestershire became a first-class county, they have produced several fine sides and considerably more outstanding cricketers than the majority of the county clubs. I hope that this book, a compendium of Gloucestershire's pictorial history, captures the flavour of those players.

Dean P. Hayes
January 1998

CHAPTER ONE

THE GRACES

century-and-a-half ago William Gilbert Grace was born into a home-grown sporting academy. HIs father and uncle were keen cricketers, his four brothers all fine players. Of the five Grace boys three, E.M., W.G. and G.F. became among the best cricketers in England, and Gilbert the greatest the game had ever seen.

Their father, Henry Mills Grace, was born on 21 February 1808 in the Somerset village of Long Ashton. Settling on a career in medicine, he was articled to a surgeon in Bristol but did not allow his studies to interfere with his love of cricket. Two or three times a week he and some friends would rise early in the morning to head for Durdham Down, a large expanse of open common ground to the north-west of the city. Here they would practise their cricket between 5 and 8 o'clock, with Henry batting right-handed but bowling and throwing in left-handed.

He later undertook further studies at the combined medical school of Guy's and St Thomas' Hospitals in London, and on qualifying embarked on the life of a country doctor. He was twenty-three when he married Martha Pocock in 1831, and though she was barely nineteen she was a perfect match for the hard-working doctor.

The Graces' first home was Downend House, on the lawn of which the doctor laid down a cricket pitch where he could practise. However, this was never going to be enough for the cricket-loving doctor and so he and his friends decided to set up their own club. They found some common land at Rodway Hill at

Afternoon tea on the lawn at The Chesnuts: Miss Grace, Mrs Dawn, the Revd J. Ward and Mrs Skelton.

Mangotsfield, about a mile east of Downend, and created their own ground. Thus was formed the Mangotsfield Cricket Club with Dr Grace and Arthur Pocock its leading players. Eventually Mangotsfield amalgamated with Coalpit Heath to become West Gloucestershire Cricket Club.

Henry and Martha Grace lived at Downend House for nineteen years, during which time Martha gave birth to eight of their nine children, five sons and four daughters. The four boys born there were Henry, the eldest (31 January 1833), Alfred (17 May 1840), Edward Mills (28 November 1841) and William Gilbert, who was born on 18 July 1848, his mother's thirty-sixth birthday. The girls were Annie, born in 1834, Fanny Hellings (1838), Alice Rose (1845) and the youngest, Elizabeth Blanche, who like W.G. was known by her second name and was born in 1847. By 1850, with their last child on the way, the Graces needed a bigger house and moved to The Chesnuts, where George Frederick ('Fred') was born on 13 December 1850 to complete the family.

Eight years after its formation the West Gloucestershire Cricket Club made history when it met William Clarke's All England XI for the first time on the field behind the Full Moon Hotel in Stokes Croft, Bristol. West Gloucestershire, captained by Dr Grace and including 'young' Henry, suffered defeat by 149 runs but nonetheless challenged the victors to a return match on the same ground the following summer. This time West Gloucestershire lost by 165 runs, but the match was memorable for the debut of fourteen-year-old E.M. Grace. However, it was another seven years before E.M. hit the headlines. His parents were visiting friends just outside Canterbury when the Kent secretary found himself a player short. He asked Dr Grace if his son would fill the gap but his reaction was that it wasn't worth bringing E.M. all the way from Bristol for just one game. Eventually the Kent secretary agreed to letting E.M. represent the MCC in the second match. He arrived on the second day just in time to bat, but was out first ball! After scoring 56 in the second innings, he then proceeded to carry his bat through the MCC innings for 192 and then captured all 10 wickets in Kent's second innings!

Although W.G. was seven years younger than E.M. he did not have to wait very long for his chance, and in 1863, when he was still only fifteen, he was included in a Bristol and District XXII against George Parr's All-England XI on Durdham Downs.

W.G. scored 126 centuries in first-class cricket, the first being for England *vs* Surrey at The Oval at the end of July 1866, a few days after his eighteenth birthday, when, going in after the third wicket had fallen at 96, he batted with such confidence that when the innings finally ended at 521 he was unbeaten with 221. A month or so later W.G. played for the 'Gentlemen of the South' against the 'Players of the South' again at The Oval, scoring 176 and taking 9 wickets for 108 runs – 7 in the Players' first innings. In two successive innings at The Oval he had scored 397 runs without losing his wicket!

It was towards the end of the 1860s that the youngest of the Graces, G.F., or Fred, as he was affectionately known, came to prominence.

Eventually the untiring efforts of Dr Grace to establish Gloucestershire cricket on a county basis culminated in a match against Surrey in June 1870. Although E.M. as well as W.G. and G.F. took part in this match, it was W.G. who led Gloucestershire to their first and well-deserved victory by 51 runs. So began the golden age of Gloucestershire county cricket during which the Grace brothers carried their team to the top of the Championship four times, including sharing the title with Nottinghamshire in 1873.

All three brothers, with W.G. as captain, played in the first England *vs* Australia Test match to be played in this country. The home side won by 5 wickets with W.G. top-scoring with 152, but both E.M. and G.F. were out in the first innings without scoring, the latter bagging a 'pair' in his only Test match.

Both E.M. and W.G. continued to enjoy many years of county cricket but Fred died tragically at the early age of thirty, the result, it is said, of sleeping in a damp bed. W.G. resigned in 1899 but E.M., the Club's first secretary, continued to hold office until two years before his death in 1911.

There is no doubt that as long as cricket is played the name of Grace will always symbolise Gloucestershire and its great contribution to the history of this wonderful game.

Dr Henry Mills Grace was born on 21 February 1808 in the Somerset village of Long Ashton, but on marrying Martha Pocock in 1831 he settled at Downend, a quiet village about 4 miles out of Bristol. He was a highly conscientious doctor and a good surgeon.

His practice extended for a 12-mile radius around Downend and he covered it on horseback, often not arriving home until after midnight. He was surgeon to the Royal Gloucestershire Reserves and did a lot of work for the underprivileged as medical officer to the Poor Law.

He was quite an enthusiast in the matter of cricket and lost no opportunity to play and watch his beloved game. In fact, his love for the game had prompted him to initiate, in 1844, the formation of the Mangotsfield Cricket Club, Mangotsfield being only a mile or so from Downend. When Mangotsfield amalgamated with Coalpit Heath two years later, the West Gloucestershire Club was formed.

He was a most abstemious man who never smoked and he drank nothing except a glass of wine with his dinner and a little whiskey and water at night. A friend of the Duke of Beaufort, he paid frequent visits to Badminton when hunting and did so right up to his death at the age of sixty-three.

Martha Grace, the daughter of George Pocock, a proprietor of a private boarding school at St Michael's Hill, Bristol. She was barely nineteen when she married Dr Henry Grace in 1831.

She grew to be the most remarkable woman, giving birth to nine children. Richard Daft once said of her: 'She knew ten times more about cricket than any lady I ever met.' Martha took as much part in the coaching of her sons as Henry ever did and closely followed their progress. She watched them play whenever she was able and was a regular visitor to Gloucestershire's matches, where batsmen, once they were dismissed, paid their respects to Mrs Grace as she sat in the stand and listened to her telling them where they had gone wrong! She always liked to be informed of her sons' performances when they were playing away from home, so they used to send her a telegram informing her of their achievements that day. She cut out all the various newspaper reports of their games and pasted them in scrapbooks.

Martha was also the author of a letter to George Parr, captain of the All England XI, in which she recommended her third son, Edward Mills Grace, for selection in the England team!

The Chesnuts, as the Graces eccentrically spelled it, was much more suitable for the large and lively family than the relatively cramped conditions of Downend House where the Graces had first lived. It was, according to contemporary description, 'a square, plain building . . . ivy creeping all over, with pretty flower garden and numerous outhouses. Walking up the carriage drive, past the lodge and old summer house, you come to the main entrance . . . beyond the orchard, some 80 yards in length, high wall on the left.' Here the beloved game of cricket was pursued with even greater vigour than before, though W.G. was only two when the family moved, so his cricket education had not yet begun. Unfortunately the house no longer exists, a British Telecom building dating from 1968 now standing on its site.

Wickets Pitched. When W.G. was of an age where he could be duly entrusted with a bat, he was initiated into the rudiments of the game under the instruction of Uncle Pocock – Mr Alfred Pocock. Certain times were set aside for cricket practice in the orchard, the elder members of the family being allowed the privilege of a quarter-of-an-hour's batting each and the younger ones five minutes. To make up their shortfall, the youngsters would steal many a quiet practice at other times, often with the aid of 'Boots' as bowler and the dogs of the house as fielders!

The West Gloucestershire team at Knowle Park, Almondsbury, 1866. Back row, left to right: the Revd H.W. Barber, H.M. Grace (father of W.G.), H. Gruning, A. Pocock (uncle of W.G.). Middle row: W.G., Henry Grace, E.M. Grace, Alfred Grace (a brotherly quartet). Front row: F. Baker, W.J. Pocock, G.F. Grace (the youngest brother), R. Brotherhood.

W.G. as a young man, aged about twenty-two. Slim and serious, he is rather self-consciously posing for the camera.

W.G. Grace and H. Jupp. The contest between the Gentlemen and the Players at The Oval on 3, 4 and 5 July 1865 was notable for the debut in the series of W.G. Grace and Harry Jupp. W.G. assisted the Gentlemen in all but one of the matches in which Jupp represented the Players – the champion ill with scarlet fever in 1867.

Of course, they were adversaries in county matches between Gloucestershire and Surrey but they were often on the same side in other first-class games for the United South of England Eleven. They were regular opening partners in one or both innings over twenty times between 1868 and 1876 in contests between the north and south.

E.M. and W.G. Grace at Sussex. If the match in which the brothers E.M. and W.G. were playing wasn't too serious, they would allow themselves a little humour. The story goes that in a village match E.M. was bowling and appealing with great regularity but without success. W.G. is reported to have told the umpire: 'Never mind my brother, he's always appealing. Now when I appeal, it is out.' A few overs elapsed before an appeal came from point and the umpire's finger was raised!

The Gloucestershire team at Brighton, 1888.

R.A. Fitzgerald's team in Canada, 1872. Back row, left to right: A. Lubbock, W.G., T.C. Patterson of the Toronto Club, C.J. Ottawa. Middle row: E. Lubbock, R.A. Fitzgerald, A. Appleby. Front row: F.P.U. Pickering, Lord Harris, A.N. Hornby, W.M. Rose, C.K. Francis.

They sailed from Liverpool on 8 August and arrived at Port Levi in Quebec on the 17th. They played their first match five days later against 'Twenty Two of Montreal'. The young Englishmen found the Canadians easy opposition and W.G. amassed a huge collection of runs; then spurred by the success of a lob-bowler in the team, he decided to prove that he could also mop up wickets.

Though he was not captain, W.G. was often required to speak at the many banquets the team attended. At Montreal he had to reply to the toast of 'The Champion Batsman of Cricketdom'. 'Gentlemen', he said, 'I beg to thank you for the honour you have done me. I never saw better bowling than I have seen today and I hope to see as good wherever I go.' At Ottawa he said: 'Gentlemen, I thank you for the honour you have done me. I never saw a better ground than I have seen today and I hope to see as good wherever I go.'

At the end of the short tour, W.G. varied his speech by saying: 'I never saw better oysters than I have seen today and I hope . . .', etc. Years later, Grace showed he had a good sense of humour when he asked: 'Shall I make one of my Canadian speeches?'

E.M. Grace (1870–96). The first of the Grace family to indicate the extraordinary cricketing talent that was to come from the three brothers, his first important game was for West Gloucestershire against the All England XI on the old Full Moon field at Fishponds, when he was only thirteen years old.

By 1862 he was one of the most dangerous batsmen in the country, and during that summer stepped in as a late replacement in the MCC side against the Gentlemen of Kent. What a replacement: he scored 192 not out and took all 10 wickets in the second innings.

In 1863 he reached his highest point as a batsman, when in all matches he topped the 3,000 run mark. He then began to qualify as a surgeon, obtaining his medical qualifications in 1865, and so to a certain extent he dropped out of the first-class cricket scene.

When Gloucestershire County Cricket Club was formed in 1871, he came back to play a leading role and was secretary right from the outset until he resigned in 1909.

In 1880 he made his one and only Test appearance at the Oval in the first Test match with Australia in this country. He continued to play for Gloucestershire until 1896 after when he channelled his energies towards club cricket.

G.F. Grace (1870–80). The youngest of five sons born to Dr Henry Mills Grace and his wife Martha, he remains the second youngest English first-class cricketer, having made his debut for the Gentlemen of England against Oxford University in 1866 at the age of 15 years 159 days. It was towards the end of this decade that young Fred, as he was affectionately known, jumped to fame. He played for the North of the Thames against the South of the Thames at Canterbury and then two years later played for the first time at Lord's when he and W.G. played for England against the MCC, for whom E.M. was a member.

His highest score for Gloucestershire was an unbeaten 180 made against Surrey at Clifton College in 1875. He made his Test debut in the first Anglo-Australian Test at the Oval in 1880 and though he collected a 'pair' and didn't bowl, he did take the historic catch off what is still reckoned the highest hit ever made. It was a magnificent running catch off a towering hit by the big-bearded Australian, George Bonnor, Fred taking the catch as the batsmen were starting their third run!

Sadly, two weeks later, on his way to a match at Winchester, he died of congestion of the lungs following a severe cold.

Uncle Pocock worked on W.G.'s stance and his footwork, and for the early years of his cricketing career insisted that he do no more than defend his wicket. He also insisted that he learned to bat the right way – left shoulder forward, head over the ball and watch the ball all the way.

In W.G.'s day all batsmen were taught to stand with one foot on either side of the crease and let the weight of the body rest mainly on the foot behind the crease. As the bowler was taking his run, his left heel was on the ground but the toe was in the air. Also, W.G. always had his bat well up in the air behind him before the bowler let go of the ball.

W.G. made batting an all-round performance. Though he revelled in hitting fast bowling, often executing the pull-drive as shown in this photograph, he developed no one special stroke by which he became famous – he used them all as the occasion demanded.

Ashley Grange, Bristol, where W.G. Grace lived for many years. The house was purchased for him from the proceeds of a 'Shilling Fund' set up in 1895 to commemorate his 100 centuries.

This eleven (which included W.G. Grace and Charlie Townsend) represented the Gentlemen against the Players at Lord's in 1899 and won decisively by an innings and 54 runs. W.G. first played for the Gentlemen against the Players in the year 1875 and in the course of his career he took part in no fewer than eighty-five Gentlemen and Player matches. He scored 6,008 runs at an average of 42.60 and took 271 wickets for under 19 runs each. He made seven centuries for the Gentlemen at Lord's, four at The Oval and one each at Brighton, Prince's (Middlesex), Scarborough and Hastings.

A display in the Museum at the County Ground, Bristol.

The ball presented to W.G. Grace to commemorate his score of 318 not out made against Yorkshire at Cheltenham in 1876.

A Coalport dessert dish in rococo design, celebrating W.G. Grace becoming the first cricketer to score a century of centuries.

The plaque on a cricket bat presented to Gloucestershire County Cricket Club by W.G.'s grandson in 1948, on the occasion of the centenary of W.G.'s birth.

The Menu Banquet Card to celebrate a century of centuries by W.G. Grace, held at the Victoria Rooms, Clifton, in June 1895.

The Bristol Century Club – the logo on the Menu Card at the Grace Banquet.

One of the last pictures ever to be taken of W.G.

The main entrance to the Lord's Cricket Ground is from St John's Wood Road through the Grace Gates, pictured here; it is used by members and their guests. The Grace Gates are the first indication of the ground's particular significance – a reminder of tradition.

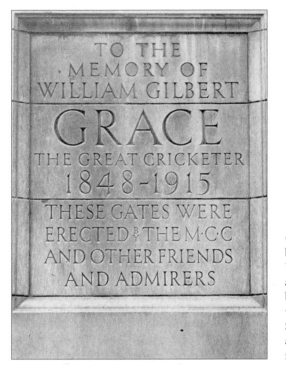

One of the massive piers of the Grace Gates bears the inscription 'to the memory of William Gilbert Grace, the great cricketer', and is surmounted by carved stumps, bats and balls grouped in the ponderous style associated with the inter-war years classical idiom. Sir Herbert Baker was the designer in 1923, and two years later his grandstand arose to fill most of the north side.

The final resting place at Elmer's End. W.G's grave was at one time neglected, but was restored, thanks to an initiative by the Forty Club. Rather surprisingly, in view of their importance to the history of the area, the Grace family graves in the churchyard are in very poor condition. No casual passer-by would realise that here lie the remains of such an important family, including two other great cricketers of the Victorian era – E.M. and G.F. Grace.

CHAPTER TWO

1870–1914

The County's greatest inspiration was, of course, W.G., though his Gloucestershire cricket was for some time by no means his most important consideration. His brothers E.M. and G.F. were both batsmen of the highest class but it was their father, Dr Grace senior, who really got Gloucestershire cricket organised after the foundation of the present club in 1870, when the county won all five matches it played.

When qualification rules were first established, in 1873, Gloucestershire and Nottinghamshire were deemed to have shared the title. Gloucestershire were led then and for the next twenty-seven seasons by W.G., who in this year scored more than 2,000 runs and took more than 100 wickets for the first time. Gloucestershire did the double over Yorkshire, beat Surrey and Sussex away and drew with them both on home ground in what was a short but unbeaten Championship season. W.G. did the 2,000 runs and 100 wickets double in each of the next five seasons, and Gloucestershire won the title outright in 1876 and 1877. E.M. Grace was a powerful all-round cricketer with a sense of fun equal to his younger brother. While batting at The Oval, E.M., then Coroner of Bristol, received a telegram demanding his prompt return to preside over an inquest. His return wire read: 'Keep corpse on ice till innings declared.' Fred Grace was a gifted, tall, commanding player cut down by lung congestion a fortnight after playing for England in the first Test at The Oval in 1880.

Like the three Graces, the County's amateur supporting cast were all useful all-rounders. Frank Townsend was the head of a famous cricketing family whose son and grandson both played for England; T.G. Matthews was a big hitter of the ball; W.R. Gilbert, who was a cousin of the Graces, was a batsman with great footwork and R.F. Miles was a slow left-arm bowler, the first in a long line of his type for Gloucestershire. The normal wicket-keeper was Arthur Bush, W.G.'s best man at his wedding, who, although a genuine number eleven batsman, helped him add 62 for the last wicket against Yorkshire at Cheltenham, enabling W.G. to reach 318 not out, which considering the strength of Yorkshire's attack was one of his best innings. In three successive innings in the course of seven days in August 1876, W.G. made 344, 177 and 318 not out, a total of 839 runs at three different venues. These scores explain to a large extent why Gloucestershire were the force they were in the 1870s.

After sharing the title again in 1880 and finishing runners-up to Lancashire the following season, Gloucestershire failed to translate brilliant individual success into team victories. They also suffered during this period from a lack of bowling penetration. W.G. had his Indian summer in 1895, scoring 1,000 runs in May. He needed to make 153 on 30 May against Middlesex at Lord's, won the toss and reached his target in late afternoon before proceeding to make 169. In all that summer he scored nine hundreds, becoming the first man to score a hundred centuries, against Somerset at Bristol in May — and 2,346 runs at an average of 51. Gloucestershire also had two other genuinely great players in Charlie Townsend and Gilbert Jessop.

In that same summer of 1895 Charlie Townsend, a tall leg-spinner who imparted really vicious spin and with his high action got bounce as well, took an almost unbelievable 122 wickets in eleven matches from the end of July. In two games against Nottinghamshire he took 16 and then 12 wickets, and against Yorkshire his haul was 15. Although, not surprisingly, he never quite equalled this, he did the double in 1898 with 130 wickets and 1,072 powerfully struck runs.

During this period Gloucestershire entertained Northamptonshire and dismissed them for 12, the smallest total for a first-class inter-county match. Gloucestershire were bowled out for 60 but Northamptonshire's first innings only lasted forty minutes. Dennett was practically unplayable and performed the hat-trick in taking 8 for 9. In Gloucestershire's second innings only Jessop and Mackenzie overcame the difficulties of the wicket, leaving Northamptonshire to get 136 to win. At the end of the second day they were 40 for 7, but rain came to their rescue with not one ball being able to be bowled on the third day.

In 1910 Gloucestershire beat Worcestershire by 94 runs, thanks almost entirely to a magnificent display of batting by Gilbert Jessop. From going in a second time 52 behind, Gloucestershire lost three wickets for 45. From this point Jessop, with his wonderful hitting, changed the entire course of the match. He scored his hundred in an hour and at the close of play was 106 not out. On the following day he continued to play brilliantly, taking his score to 165. He obtained his runs in two hours out of 215, his superb innings including six sixes and twenty fours. Left with 210 to win on a damaged pitch, the home side never looked like getting the runs against the fine bowling of Dennett and Parker.

Gilbert Jessop was the greatest hitter in cricket history. Compact and very strong, he leapt at bowlers of all types from his famous crouching stance and savaged them with rapid footwork followed by a brutal but basically orthodox attack. He hit 53 hundreds in a career, averaging in these innings an amazing 82.7 runs an hour. He captained Gloucestershire from 1900 to 1912 and played his last game in 1914. The Club's position during this season was extremely grave and it was feared that Gloucestershire would have to be wound up. At a Special General Meeting on 27 October, in Bristol, it was decided to continue for another year. No fixtures were to be made for 1915 and the professionals were not to be paid so they could qualify for other Counties.

In that first season of 1870 Gloucestershire only played three matches against first-class opposition and won all three. In the first at Durdham Downs on 2, 3 and 4 June, Surrey were beaten by 51 runs, with W.G., who made 26 and 25 with the bat, having match figures of 9 for 92. In the return match at the Oval Gloucestershire won by an innings and 129 runs, with W.G. making 143 and Frank Townsend 89 in the County's total of 336. In the third match against the MCC at Lord's, W.G. made 172 out of Gloucestershire's total of 276 as the home side were beaten by an innings and 86 runs.

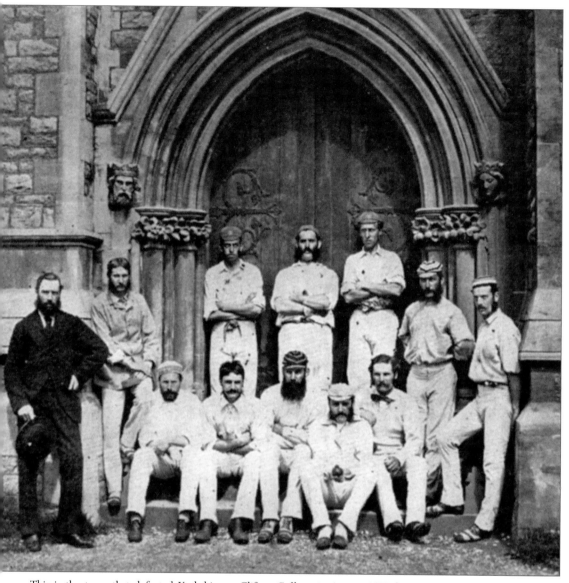

This is the team that defeated Yorkshire at Clifton College in August 1874 by an innings and 78 runs. Front row, left to right: F.J. Crook, F. Townsend, W.G. Grace, G.F. Grace, R.F. Miles. Back row: Pullin (umpire), T.G. Matthews; E.C.B. Ford; J.A. Bush, R.E. Bush, E.M. Grace, E.M. Knapp.

After sharing the Championship with Nottinghamshire in 1873, this season Gloucestershire were outright champions. Despite the arduous tour to Australia during the winter, W.G. averaged 85 in county matches and took 60 wickets at 11.53 runs apiece.

'THE CHAMPION'

W.G.Grace (1870–99). W.G. Grace was surely the greatest player the game has ever known or will know. Up to 1863 W.G. was steadily building a local reputation. In that year he took a step forward when he played for the first time against professional bowling of the highest calibre, when the All England XI came down to play twenty-two men of Bristol on Durdham Down. In 1866, when he was only eighteen years old, he played his first major innings, making 224 for All England against Surrey, and at the same time he was given time off to run a hurdle race at Crystal Palace. Even in those early years he seemed to be breaking convention.

In 1868 he played what he always thought was his best innings, when he scored an all-run 134 at Lord's on a terrible wicket out of the Gentlemen's 201 against the Players. He then scored two hundreds for the South in a match against the North of the Thames at Canterbury, the first time such a feat had been achieved since William Lambert at Lord's in 1817.

Soon to become internationally famous, Grace toured Canada and the United States in 1872, where he was hailed as 'the Champion Batsman of Cricketdom and a monarch in his might'. In 1874 Grace scored 1,000 runs and took 100 wickets in eleven consecutive matches – a phenomenal feat. His best year as a bowler was 1875 when he captured 191 wickets at 12.92 runs apiece.

In 1876 he scored 2,622 runs at an average of 62.42, and in the month of August he scored in three successive innings 344 for the MCC against Kent at Canterbury, 177 against Nottinghamshire at Clifton and then his highest score for Gloucestershire, 318 not out against Yorkshire at Cheltenham.

In 1880 he hit 152 at the Oval in the first match in this country between England and Australia. He was thirty-two years old when he played in his first Test and had already scored some 20,000 first-class runs, the record for a debutant. There are suggestions that because he was putting on weight and was very heavy for so young a man, he may have just passed his best. Nevertheless, over the next nineteen years he scored 1,098 Test runs at an average of 32.29, though he had to battle against his increasing size for the rest of his cricket life.

In what may be termed the second part of his career, a climax was reached in 1895. In May he scored 1,016 runs at an average of 112.88, including 288 against Somerset to become the first man ever to score a hundred first-class hundreds. In 1896 he was still in good form, scoring 2,135 runs at 42.70, but after that the years began to tell on him.

In 1899 W.G. split with Gloucestershire. The Cricket Committee had heard of his offer of employment with the London County Club which was just being formed at Crystal Palace. The County Committee wrote to W.G. asking which matches he intended to play for Gloucestershire. He was furious because he had played in all Gloucestershire's first-class matches in the season so far. Grace replied to the committee by sending his resignation and inviting them to choose teams for all future games.

In a first-class career which stretched from 1865 to 1908 he scored, according to Wisden, 54,896 runs and took 2,876 wickets. W.G.'s record should include all other games in which he collected about 45,000 more runs and 4,500 wickets. If these were added up, they would reach totals never imagined before, some 100,000 runs and over 7,000 wickets.

'The Champion', W.G. Grace.

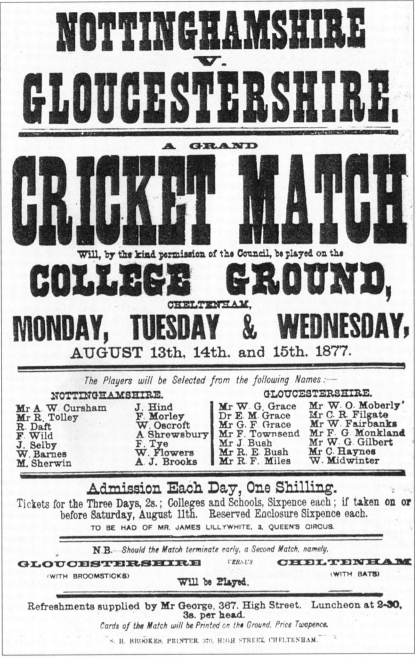

This is the poster advertising the Gloucestershire *vs* Nottinghamshire game at Cheltenham College in 1877. It contains a number of points of interest. Mr James Lillywhite was allowed a sum of money to run the early games in Cheltenham. The Nottinghamshire team contained two amateurs and nine professionals, while Gloucestershire played ten amateurs and one professional.

It was the custom in the early days of county cricket to put on a throwing contest or perhaps another match if a game finished early. In the match that followed the County match, Gloucestershire made 299 with broomsticks, E.M. Grace 104 and Midwinter 58, to which Cheltenham, using bats, replied with 50 for 2 before time ran out!

William Woof (1878–1902). Gloucester-born William Woof was the County's second full-time professional after Midwinter. He first played in 1878 and the great Gloucestershire tradition of left-arm spin bowlers began. In 1882 W.G. Grace recommended Woof to the Lord's ground staff and there he remained for four seasons, making a name for himself in MCC matches. In one match against Nottinghamshire he and his opening partner, Rylott, delivered 64 balls at the start of the Trent Bridge side's innings without a single run being scored from the bat. Woof dismissed three players in the space of 5 balls including England players Billy Barnes and Wilfred Flowers. In seasons 1884 and 1885 he dismissed over 100 batsmen and, during the latter, was appointed coach at Cheltenham College, which limited the number of games he was able to play for the County.

He retired initially from the first-class game in 1894, although he played his last game for Gloucestershire in 1902 against the Australians on the Cheltenham College Ground. Woof kept his position at Cheltenham for forty years, where on his retirement he received £1,200 as a testimonial from past and present Cheltonians.

Fred Roberts (1887–1905). Fred Roberts made a sensational start to his Gloucestershire career, for in his first match against Yorkshire at Dewsbury he took seven wickets in each innings for an aggregate of 171 runs. He bowled 138 overs in the match but was still on the losing side. Also in his first season of 1887 he took 5 for 8 as Kent were bowled out for 28.

He didn't possess great skill as a batsman but quite often would keep up his end in the case of an emergency. In the 1903 fixture against Sussex nine Gloucestershire wickets had fallen. Roberts then helped Brown put on 104 for the last wicket. Brown was eventually out for 155, Roberts' contribution being 11 not out!

His best season with the ball was 1901 when he dismissed 118 batsmen at an average of under 23 runs apiece. Able to get a lot of work on the ball both ways, the left-handed bowler played for ten seasons before a facing batsman was given out lbw. After retiring from first-class cricket in 1905, with 963 wickets to his credit, he was appointed to the first-class umpires list and stood regularly until the outbreak of the First World War.

1888 team. Back row, left to right: J. Smith (scorer), J.R. Painter, W.W.F. Pullen, F.G. Roberts, J.H. Brain, W.A. Woof, the Revd E. Peake, H.F.B. Champain. Front row: O.G. Radcliffe, E.M. Grace, W.G. Grace (captain), F. Townsend, H.V. Page.

After sharing the 1880 Championship with Nottinghamshire and finishing runners-up to Lancashire the following summer, Gloucestershire's best season up to 1895 was in 1888 when they finished fourth, winning seven of their sixteen matches. The season, though, was notable for the acquisition of a piece of land at Ashley Down on which was founded Gloucestershire's headquarters. They remain there today.

1894 team. Back row, left to right: J. Smith (scorer), J.R. Painter, F.G. Roberts, W.G. Grace jnr, C.L. Townsend, J.H. Board. Middle row: G.L. Jessop, R.W. Rice, W.G. Grace (captain), J.J. Ferris, H.V. Page. Front row: H. Wrathall, H.H. Francis.

In the period 1890–4 Gloucestershire were a poor side and finished bottom of the County Championship in 1891, 1893 and 1894, seasons in which W.G. failed to score a century!

Charlie Townsend (1893–1922). The son of Frank Townsend, who had played for Gloucestershire in the great days of the Graces, he entered Clifton College at the age of fourteen, and in three years captured 199 wickets at 10.52 each.

He made his County debut at the age of sixteen, and in his second match against Somerset at Cheltenham performed the hat-trick, with all his victims being stumped by wicket-keeper Brain. It was 1895 when Townsend made his mark in county cricket, taking 124 wickets at a cost of only 12.58 runs each. His best performance came against Nottinghamshire at Trent Bridge, where he had match figures of 16 for 122, and in the return fixture at Cheltenham he took 13 for 110. After this there came a decline in his bowling but he developed into one of the best left-handed batsmen in the country. In 1897 he scored his maiden century against Yorkshire and in 1898 he performed the double, finishing the season with 1,270 runs and 145 wickets; he was named the *Wisden* Cricketer of the Year. In 1899 he scored 2,440 runs, including his highest career score of 224 not out against Essex, and not surprisingly made his Test debut against Australia at Lord's.

After 1900 he played little cricket owing to his appointment as a solicitor and later Official Receiver at Stockton-on-Tees. In 1906 he made a notable appearance for Gloucestershire, scoring 214 against Warwickshire, and in 1909 scored 129 out of 169 in two hours at Cheltenham in the match against Noble's Australians. He continued to play after the war, and in 1920 was involved in a remarkable game against Somerset. Having been bowled out for 22 in their first innings, Gloucestershire were set 274 to win and, with Townsend scoring 84 out of 119 in 75 minutes, won by 4 wickets! One of the most brilliant of W.G.'s finds, he played his last game in 1922.

1895 team. Back row, left to right: H. Wrathall, J.R. Painter, J. Smith (scorer), W.H. Murch, F.G. Roberts. Middle row: E.M. Grace, A.T.H. Newnham, W.G. Grace (captain), J.J. Ferris, S.A.P. Kitcat. Front row: W. Troup, J.H. Board, H.W. Brown.

In one of the most dramatic seasons in the County's history, W.G. Grace in his forty-seventh year became the first batsman ever to make 1,000 runs in the month of May, having scored 1,016 runs at an average of 112.88 between 9 and 30 May. Only twice since has this feat been achieved, by Walter Hammond in 1927 and Lancashire's Charlie Hallows in 1928. During the course of May W.G. scored 288 against Somerset at Bristol to record his hundredth first-class century, and with Charlie Townsend taking 124 wickets in his first full season the county moved up to fourth in the Championship.

1898 team. In what was W.G.'s last full season, in which he scored over 1,500 runs at an average of around 40, the County finished third. It was their highest position for seventeen years and another thirty-two years before it was bettered. Charlie Townsend, who took 9 for 48 against Middlesex at Lord's, did the double – scoring 1,270 runs and capturing 145 wickets. Not surprisingly he was named as one of *Wisden's* Cricketers of the Year.

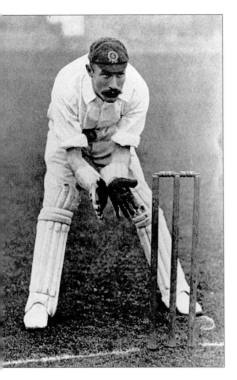

Jack Board (1891–1914). Jack Board kept wicket in an era when the gloves were on the small side and the pads paper weight. He was aided by the slow left-arm spinners of George Dennett and the guile of Charlie Townsend. Batsmen would regularly make attacking sorties down the wicket only to find themselves in no-man's land when the ball turned. It is no wonder that Board claimed 317 stumpings in his Gloucestershire career.

Jack Board was a protégé of W.G. Grace and as the years passed he began to develop his batting. In 1900 he passed the 1,000 run mark for the first of what was to be six seasons and hit the highest score of his career, 214 against Somerset at Bristol.

He kept wicket for England on six occasions, all against South Africa between 1898 and 1906. In 1911, when Gloucestershire played Hampshire at Southampton, the home side scored 594 for 6 declared, yet Jack Board didn't concede a single bye! He held his position as Gloucestershire's first-choice wicket-keeper right up to the outbreak of the First World War. He played in 430 matches and claimed 1,016 victims, as well as scoring 13,092 runs.

Harry Wrathall (1894–1907). Cheltenham-born opening batsman Harry Wrathall began his Gloucestershire career in 1894 and over the next fourteen seasons gave the County great service. He had a reputation as a somewhat stonewalling batsman, and before the turn of the century had been involved in two lengthy partnerships for the ninth and tenth wickets. In 1898 he helped W.S.A. Brown put on 156 for the ninth wicket against Warwickshire at Edgbaston, and the following season added 106 with Jack Board for the tenth wicket against Surrey at The Oval.

In 1903 he and Theodore Fowler put on 277 for the first wicket in the match against London County at Crystal Palace, with Wrathall's share being 160. His top score for Gloucestershire was an innings of 176 made against Somerset, and when this fine professional batsman played his last game for the County in 1907 he had scored 10,289 runs at an average of 23.01.

'THE CROUCHER'

Gilbert Jessop (1894–1914). In 1895, a year after making his Gloucestershire debut, Jessop began to establish his reputation. At Cheltenham he hit 63 out of 65 in less than thirty minutes against Yorkshire and took 5 for 13 against Lancashire – the first of his bowling successes. At this time Jessop was a schoolmaster at Beccles School, for whom he hit 1,058 runs at an average of 132 and took 100 wickets at a cost of less than 2.5 runs apiece!

By 1897 Jessop had become one of the greatest players of the day, scoring 1,219 runs and taking 116 wickets. That summer saw him score two centuries of note. The first was 140 for Cambridge University, whom he was to captain in 1899 against the Philadelphians, in just ninety-five minutes, followed by 101 not out in forty minutes in the match against Yorkshire at Harrogate. Not surprisingly he was chosen as the *Wisden* Cricketer of the Year.

When Jessop was selected for his first Test match in 1899 he was still at Cambridge, though a year later, following the retirement of W.G. Grace, he was appointed captain of Gloucestershire. The cares of leading his County didn't seem to affect him; he reached three figures in both innings of the match against Yorkshire and scored 179 in 105 minutes against Sussex at Hove. He ended the summer with 2,210 runs and took 104 wickets, including 8 for 29 against Essex. In 1901 his aggregate score was 2,323 runs, including 157 out of 201 in an hour against the West Indies!

Jessop played in eighteen Tests for England between 1899 and 1909, and at The Oval in 1902 he earned everlasting fame. Conditions favoured the bowlers and England, set 273 to win in their final innings, were 48 for 5 when Jessop marched out to join F.S. Jackson. He hit 104 out of a partnership of 139 in only 77 minutes, paving the way for a one wicket win by England. Also in 1902 he achieved the highest score of his career, 286 against Sussex at Hove.

Jessop at his best could hit runs from any ball, no matter how good it was. Though only 5 ft 7 ins tall and weighing 11 stone, he was extremely powerful, quick to move and with a marvellous eye. As he shaped to play he bent low, earning himself the title of 'The Croucher'. He was equally ready if the ball was pitched up or short – he seemed to hurl himself towards the pitch of the ball and fling his bat at it. He was such an impressive batsman that within thirty minutes he could change the course of a game. He was such a unique cricketer that no one in the game scored at such a rate and with such success. His figures show that his centuries were scored at an average of 82.70 runs per hour and his five double centuries at slightly less than 100.

Jessop's greatness wasn't just limited to his batsmanship. For a number of years he was highly thought of as a fast bowler, showing surprising stamina for a man of his pace. He was also an excellent fielder, batsmen loath to take the chance of a run to him no matter how deep he was!

'The Croucher', Gilbert Jessop.

Charlie Townsend, Gilbert Jessop and Harry Wrathall stand in front of the scoreboard at Bristol, showing details at the fall of Jessop's wicket in the match against the West Indies in June 1900. Though the match was not given first-class status, Jessop put on 201 in an hour with Townsend, of which he himself made 157.

Display of bats. From top to bottom: Bat made by Brownings of Fishponds, Bristol, believed to have been used for practice in the 1830s; T.G. Matthews (1870–6) used this bat to become the first player to score a double century for Gloucestershire when he made 201 against Surrey at Clifton College in 1871; C.L. Townsend (1893–1922) scored over 1,000 runs in the 1899 season with this bat.

This is thought to be the first time a chart of scoring shots was published. It refers to Gilbert Jessop's innings of 93 runs made in the first South Africa Test match at Lord's in 1907. Jessop and Braund of Somerset put on 145 runs in seventy minutes towards an England total of 428. G.A. Faulkner caught Jessop on the boundary when he had scored 93. That year the South Africans beat Gloucestershire at the County Ground, Bristol, by an innings and 38 runs.

A set of County Cricketers cigarette cards.

A set of Wills' cigarette cards.

1901 team. Back row, left to right: F.G. Roberts, H. Wrathall, T. Langdon, H.J. Huggins, J.H. Board. Seated: T.H. Fowler, S.A.P. Kitcat, G.L. Jessop (captain), C.O.H. Sewell, H.S. Goodwin. Seated on ground: A.J. Paish.

A disappointing season for the County who finished fourteenth in the Championship, just one place above bottom club Derbyshire. Gilbert Jessop scored 2,323 runs, including a century in fifty-seven minutes, in the match against Middlesex at Lord's. He also scored 233 out of 318 in two and a half hours for an All England XI against Yorkshire at Lord's.

1903 team. Back row, left to right: E.J. Spry, H. Wrathall, W.H. Hale, E.G. Dennett, T. Langdon, H.J. Huggins. Front row: J.H. Board, S.A.P. Kitcat, G.L. Jessop (captain), T.H. Fowler, F.G. Roberts.

In yet another poor season for the County Gilbert Jessop, in adding 320 with Jack Board for the sixth wicket against Sussex at Hove, scored 200 in two hours before finally being dismissed for 286. W.G. Grace scored 150 for London CCC against Gloucestershire at the Crystal Palace and became the first President of the English Bowling Association. It was also a summer when Arthur O. Jones of Nottinghamshire scored 296 at Trent Bridge – the highest score made against the County.

om Langdon (1900–14). Despite a modest start which
esulted in the Brighton-born batsman losing his first team
lace in 1906, he wasn't deterred. The following summer he
`as second only to his captain Gilbert Jessop in terms of total
uns scored, with 1,219. Showing the full range of his talents, a
ogged defence and an ability to score runs freely from a wide
ariety of strokes, Langdon produced a performance that shook
ɪe strong visiting South African side. The tourists felt the full
ɔrce of an opening stand of 95 inside an hour at the start of the
ɪatch from Langdon and his opening partner Jack Board.
ɪnfortunately for Gloucestershire the rest of the batting didn't
ome up to scratch, and when they went out in their second
ɪnnings they were 189 runs adrift. Although Gloucestershire
`ere dismissed for 151 and lost the match by an innings and
8 runs, Tom Langdon gave a superb display by carrying his bat
ɔr 78 runs. He was the only player on the county circuit to
erform such a feat that season.

   Though the war curtailed his first-class career, Langdon had
roved an extremely valuable team member, often holding the
ɪloucestershire batting together.

Harry Huggins (1901–21). Oxford-born Harry Huggins had
turned twenty-four before his residential qualification allowed
him to appear in county cricket in 1901. In those early days he
relied mainly on swing, but by the following season he began to
concentrate more on length and spin and turned in some
remarkable performances with the ball. In May at Hove against
Sussex he took 7 for 17 off 21.5 overs, and three months later
similar figures, 7 for 37 off 21.1 overs, in the match at
Worcester.

   As his career unfolded he looked as if he would develop into an
all-rounder and was moved up the batting order in 1904.
However, it was this season that he produced his best bowling
figures for the County, 9 for 34 against Sussex at Bristol. Eight of
his victims were clean bowled, the other being caught and
bowled. C.B. Fry, the Sussex captain, spoke from personal
experience when he said that Harry Huggins was as 'equal to any
bowler that Sussex played against during that summer'.

   He put on weight in the latter years of his career and his
brilliant performances with the ball lessened. He played his last
game for the County in 1921, when he became the County
scorer, a position he held for several seasons.

1904 team. Back row, left to right: H.J. Huggins, E.G. Dennett, J.H. Board, T. Langdon, A.S. Sellick, E.J. Spry. Front row: F.E. Thomas, R.T. Godsell, G.L. Jessop (captain), S.A.P. Kitcat, H. Wrathall.

There was a slight improvement this season with five out of eighteen matches being won and ninth position achieved in a Championship of fifteen counties. Two notable individual performances this summer saw Harry Huggins take 9 for 34 against Sussex at Bristol and Gilbert Jessop score another double century in 140 minutes against Nottinghamshire at Trent Bridge.

1905 team. Back row, left to right: H.J. Huggins, E.G. Dennett, J.H. Board, T. Langdon, P.T. Mills, W.H. Hale. Front row: F.E. Thomas, R.T. Godsell, G.L. Jessop (captain), L.D. Brownlee, H. Wrathall.

The most outstanding result in a summer which saw the County move up one place was a thrilling one run win over the eventual County Championship winners Yorkshire, at Bristol. Gilbert Jessop hit another double century in the match against Somerset at the County Ground in 130 minutes and George Dennett came to the fore, taking 131 wickets.

Percy Mills (1902–29). Not the luckiest of bowlers in his early years with the county, Percy Mills changed from medium-pace right-arm seam bowling to bowling off-spinners and cutters, and took many more wickets.

For some years he shared the attack with Charlie Parker. He would often keep the runs down while Charlie took the majority of wickets. However, in 1926 he claimed 101 victims including 6 for 26 from 17 overs in the match against Derbyshire – a great example of unerring accuracy. That season, the Gloucestershire Committee in its search for new talent set up a Cricket Nursery at the Fry's Ground. Percy Mills (although he played until 1929) was thought to be nearing the end of his playing career and was asked to be coach.

In 1928, at the age of forty-five, he took five wickets in the match against Somerset without conceding a run – only the fourth time that the feat had been performed.

One of the mainstays of the Gloucestershire side, his bowling brought him 824 wickets at an average of 25.16 runs each. After a spell as coach at Radley College, he became a first-class umpire before returning to the County Ground at Bristol to assist in the coaching of the juniors.

George Dennett (1903–26). George Dennett was a slow left-arm bowler who relied on accuracy and gentle spin. He had a quick arm action with the most peculiar of habits: he used to watch the ball leave his hand!

In 1906 he achieved the feat of taking all 10 wickets in an innings. The match was played at Bristol, the opponents were Essex and George finished with 10 for 40. In 1907, in the match against Northamptonshire at Gloucester, the visitors were dismissed for 12 runs – still the lowest score in first-class cricket. George Dennett took 8 for 9 including the hat-trick. In the second innings he took 7 for 12. The 15 wickets that Dennett took were all in the space of one day but Gloucestershire didn't win the match, rain preventing any play on the third day. That year he became the first Gloucestershire player to take over 200 wickets in a season.

In the match against Kent at Dover in 1912 he removed the home side's last six batsmen in just 20 balls without conceding a run and in 1913 took 9 for 36 against Surrey including the hat-trick.

Only Charlie Parker and Tom Goddard have taken more than Dennett's 2,082 wickets for the County.

1906 team. George Dennett had an outstanding season, his 160 wickets in the Championship helping Gloucestershire to a respectable ninth place. In the 9 wicket win over Essex at Bristol Dennett took all 10 wickets for a cost of only 40 runs, and followed this up in the second innings by obtaining 5 more wickets to finish with 15 for 98.

1907 team. Back row, left to right: C.S. Barnett, T. Langdon, E.G. Dennett, P.H. Ford, A.E. Winstone, C.W.L. Parker, P.T. Mills. Front row: J.H. Board, C.E.B. Champain, G.L. Jessop (captain), F.M. Luce, H.J. Huggins.

Despite winning eight games, two more than in 1906, the County dropped down one position in the Championship. The outstanding feature of Gloucestershire's cricket that season was Dennett's bowling, when with practically everything depending upon him he rarely failed his side, dismissing 184 batsmen in County Championship matches. In all matches he was the only cricketer to take 200 wickets and the first Gloucestershire player to do so. In the match against Northamptonshire at Gloucester, the visitors were put out for 12 and Dennett took 8 wickets for 9 runs including the hat-trick.

Alf Dipper (1908–32). Alf Dipper scored the majority of his
runs on the leg-side. It is reputed that at his home in Deerhurst
there was a bed of nettles on the leg-side of the field on which
they played. Young Alfred soon realised the value of hitting the
ball in that direction and, at County level, not even seven
fieldsmen around him could prevent Dipper from scoring a
fairly regular 3 runs an over.

For many seasons he was the sheet anchor of the
Gloucestershire side, carrying his bat eleven times through a
County innings, that was two more than the great W.G.
In 1923 he topped the 2,000 run mark for the first of what
was to be five times and hit the highest score of his career, an
unbeaten 252 against Glamorgan at Cheltenham College. His
best season with the bat was 1928 when he scored 2,358 runs.

Fifty-three centuries and 27,948 runs tell their own story of
Alf Dipper's contribution to Gloucestershire cricket. A shy
and thoughtful cricketer, he was second only to Walter
Hammond for many years in the number of runs scored by an
individual for the County.

Harry Smith (1912–35). Seen here, left, going out to bat with
Ken Stephens, Harry Smith made his debut for Gloucestershire in
1912, though it was another couple of years before he replaced
Jack Board behind the stumps on a regular basis. He went on to
play in 393 matches for Gloucestershire, until 1932 when illness
forced him to retire. However, three years later he received an
unexpected recall to the side.

Harry Smith developed into quite a useful batsman and was
often Alf Dipper's right-hand man in times of crisis. In 1919 he
hit centuries in both innings of the match against Hampshire at
Southampton, 120 and 102 not out. In 1927, when
Gloucestershire played Surrey at The Oval, Smith didn't concede
a single bye as the home side totalled 557 for 7 declared. The
following year he appeared in his only Test match against the
West Indies at Lord's. Smith had also played football for both
Bristol Rovers and Bolton Wanderers and was a physical fitness
enthusiast – often taking long walks before his breakfast in
readiness for stumping many a frustrated batsman.

A career total of 13,330 runs shows evidence of his reliability as
a batsman, and 705 victims (441 caught and 264 stumped) puts
him fourth in the list of dismissals by Gloucestershire wicket-
keepers.

Charlie Parker (1903–35). Though his sporting inclinations leant towards golf rather than cricket, he joined the Tewkesbury Cricket Club, where he met Alf Dipper and other prominent members of the Club who also served on the County Committee.

He made his debut against London Counties and W.G. in 1903, though over the next four years he only played a handful of games. In fact, when he started to play on a more regular basis in 1907, he had only played in two first-class games and taken one wicket!

After starting his career as a seam bowler, he changed to bowling as a spinner and from 1920 to 1935 took 100 wickets or more each season. There were many times in that period when he would bowl seamers with the new ball and then switch to bowling spinners.

In 1921 he took 164 wickets and was chosen for his one and only Test match at Old Trafford, which was spoiled by rain. He returned to Bristol to play for Gloucestershire and took all 10 wickets for 79 as Somerset were beaten by one wicket.

In 1922 in his benefit match against Yorkshire at Bristol he hit the stumps with five successive deliveries, although one was a no-ball! His final figures were 9 for 36 though Gloucestershire lost the game by 4 wickets. He ended the season with 206 wickets and was chosen as a *Wisden* Cricketer of the Year.

Parker performed the hat-trick on six occasions and in 1924 did it twice in the Middlesex fixture. In 1925 he took 222 wickets, including 17 for 56 against Essex, and still holds the record for most wickets in three successive innings, 26!

After taking 3,170 wickets for Gloucestershire from 25,307 overs in 602 matches, he retired to join the first-class umpire's list.

CHAPTER THREE

BETWEN THE WARS

Photo : Western Daily Press

Gloucestershire team v Australia 1930

R. G. Ford (12th man); B. S. Bloodworth (Scorer); A. E. Dipper
E. J. Stephens; C. C. Dacre; R. A. Sinfield; W. R. Hammond
W. L. Neale; C. J. Barnett; H. Smith
C. W. L. Parker; B. H. Lyon; F. J. Seabrook; T. W. Goddard

Gloucestershire cricket for most of the period between the wars was dominated by the wonderful all-round work of Walter Hammond — a brilliant fielder anywhere who became a specialist slip as good as any in history, and also a medium-paced bowler of whom E.W. Swanton wrote: 'If he had never made a run he might have been a second Tate.' Above all, though, Hammond was a brilliant batsman with both the ability to play every attacking stroke with perfect balance and tremendous power, and discipline to restrict himself to 'percentage' shots.

Until he began to appear regularly, the county relied mainly on a group of trusted professionals: the dependable opening batsman Alf Dipper; the wicket-keeper Harry Smith; the slow-medium Percy Mills and the two left-arm spinners George Dennett and Charlie Parker. Dennett, who took 2,147 wickets, is one of the unsung heroes of county cricket. Unlike him, Parker was selected for England — but only once in 1921 — scant reward for a superbly consistent performer who took more wickets in first-class cricket than anyone except Wilfred Rhodes and 'Tich' Freeman. Parker was unfailingly deadly on a 'sticky', quite remorselessly accurate and both flatter and quicker than most of his type.

In 1922 some of the Gloucestershire scorecards made curious reading. In the game against Hampshire at Bristol, no fewer than 14 of the visitors' wickets which fell were clean bowled. And in Derbyshire's second innings at Gloucester, Charlie Parker in taking 9 for 87 hit the stumps seven times. Also at Gloucester in the match against Worcestershire, Parker and Mills bowled unchanged throughout, disposing of the visitors for 58 (Mills 6 for 28, Parker 4 for 22) and 52 (Parker 7 for 28 and Mills 3 for 15) to help their side to victory by an innings and 92 runs.

The Packer's Ground at Bristol was the scene of a remarkable match at the end of the 1924 season. Victory for the visitors Middlesex would have assured them of the championship, and after dismissing Gloucestershire for 31 they certainly seemed to be on their way to their goal. But fine bowling by Charlie Parker, who took 7 for 30, including a hat-trick, kept the Middlesex lead down to 43. Again the Gloucestershire batsmen, with one notable exception, failed in their second innings. Walter Hammond, coming in at 8 for 1, played a magnificent innings of 174 not out in four hours ten minutes, enabling the county to declare at 294 for 9. It was Parker who did most of the damage in the Middlesex second innings. Again he did the hat-trick, again he took 7 wickets — for 101 runs — and Middlesex were dismissed for 190, losing the match and the Championship.

Several new talents were added during the 1920s, notably another great spin bowler, Tom Goddard, one of the best of all off-spinners, who in his youth had been a moderate faster bowler; Charlie Barnett, a dashing opening batsman who quickly and rightly became exceptionally popular with crowds all round the country; Reg Sinfield, a stubborn right-handed batsman with a very different approach, and a deceptively bland-looking medium-paced bowler, and Bev Lyon, whose truly dynamic captaincy enlivened county cricket from his first year in charge in 1929. Gloucestershire finished fourth that year, but would probably have won if they had not lost thrilling matches to Nottinghamshire by only six runs and Sussex by only one. The Club tried unsuccessfully at this period to persuade the Advisory County Committee to allow more points for a win and fewer for a lead on first innings. Gloucestershire in 1929, the first season in which all counties played an equal number of games, won fifteen of their twenty-eight matches, three more than anyone else, yet finished three points behind Lancashire.

In 1930 the County game against the touring Australians at Bristol ended in a tie, this great match being discussed in greater detail later in the book (p. 71).

Gloucestershire were runners-up again in 1931. It was sad that they had come so close without getting a title, and not until the later years of the decade did they threaten the leaders again. One of the county's most outstanding victories which created something of a sensation was the defeat of the formidable South African side by 87 runs at Cheltenham in 1935. The result was completely unexpected as Gloucestershire were languishing at the foot of the County Championship. The tourists had opened their visit to England with four consecutive wins and were unbeaten, having been the first South African touring side to beat England in a Test in this country. Chasing 289 to win on the last day, they were bowled out for 201 with Reg Sinfield taking 5 for 31, giving him match figures of 8 for 72, and with a century in Gloucestershire's first innings he was certainly man of the match.

The dour left-hander Jack Crapp and the more exuberant stroke-player George Emmett had settled into the side before 1939, and both in time were to play for England.

1922 team. Back row, left to right: H. Smith, W.R. Hammond, J.G.W.T. Beasant, J. Howman, P.T. Mills, A.E. Dipper. Front row: E.G. Dennett, M.A. Green, Sir F.G. Robinson (captain), H.A. Reed, C.W.L. Parker.

After finishing seventh the previous season Gloucestershire slipped to thirteenth, the batting apart from Alf Dipper, who scored 117 and 103 against Sussex, being totally unreliable. Charlie Parker took 206 wickets in all games and 195 for the County at 13.17 runs each, and in his Benefit game against Yorkshire he hit the stumps with five consecutive balls, though one was a no-ball. He was well supported by Percy Mills and George Dennett, but with so few runs to bowl at the County suffered seventeen defeats from their twenty-eight games.

1924 team. Back row, left to right: H. Smith, N.F.C. Hobbs, A.E. Dipper, J.G.W.T. Beasant, T.W.J. Goddard, W.R. Hammond, P.T. Mills, B.S. Bloodworth. Front row: E.G. Dennett, B.H. Lyon, D.C. Robinson (captain), F.G. Rogers, C.W.L. Parker.

Now possessing a nucleus of gifted professionals and a new captain in Lt-Col. D.C. Robinson, the County advanced to sixth position. It was a wet summer and only Dipper and the fast emerging Hammond, who hit a masterly unbeaten 174 against Middlesex, showed any consistency with the bat. Charlie Parker revelled in the conditions, taking 184 wickets in the Championship at a cost of 13.51 runs apiece. He performed the hat-trick on three occasions, including both innings of the Middlesex game at Packer's. Tom Goddard also achieved the feat against Sussex at Eastbourne.

'A Genius of his Time'

Walter Hammond (1920–51). Born in Dover on 19 June 1903, Walter Hammond played his first game in the Championship in 1920, though it was 1923 before he played consistently for the County. In 1924 at Bristol, on a terrible wicket in the match against Middlesex, he amazed everyone. Gloucestershire had been dismissed for only 31 and Middlesex themselves could only muster 74. In Gloucestershire's second innings Hammond scored a majestic unbeaten 174 in only four hours, enabling his side to go on and win the match.

Hammond's class was obvious but many judges thought him too headstrong, playing too many shots! This theory was certainly dispelled at Old Trafford in the August of 1925. Hammond scored 250 not out against the pace of Ted McDonald, the off-spin of Cecil Parkin and the leg spin of Dick Tyldesley.

During the winter of 1925–6 he was bitten by a mosquito and contracted an illness for which the Caribbean doctors had no answer. He was shipped back to England and spent the majority of the 1926 season in hospital.

He returned to English cricket a great batsman – a remarkable achievement considering a year earlier he had been close to death.

In the month of May 1927 he scored 1,000 runs in only twenty-two days and ended the season with 2,522 runs in the Championship at an average of 72.05. In 1928 he scored 2,474 runs at 82.46 and in the match against Surrey held 10 catches, an achievement that will stay in the record books forever. In all first-class matches that summer Hammond made 78 catches, yet another record for a fieldsman other than a wicket-keeper. This was also the season that he performed his best bowling, taking 9 for 23 against Worcestershire.

In 1928–9 he toured Australia in Percy Chapman's side. He outshone everyone, amassing 905 runs, still the most runs in a Test series by an English batsman. At Sydney he scored 251; at Melbourne 200 and at Adelaide 119 and 177. His batting average for the Test series was a mere 113.12! Both aggregate and average remain a record in Australia.

In 1935 he became the quickest compiler of a hundred hundreds, having scored his first century in 1923. He was at his best three years later both in the County Championship and at Test level. For Gloucestershire he scored seven hundreds in eight successive innings, his highest score being 271 against Lancashire at Bristol. For England at Lord's he scored a masterly 240, after Australian paceman Ernie McCormick had blasted out Charlie Barnett, Len Hutton and Bill Edrich for just 31 runs.

He went on to play in eighty-five Test matches, scoring 7,249 runs at an average of 58.45. For Gloucestershire, he scored 33,664 runs at 57.05 and a highest score of 317 made against Nottinghamshire at Gloucester in 1936.

After remarrying, he left these shores to start a new life in Durban but his life in South Africa seemed dogged by bad luck. He invested all his life savings in the motor trade but within a few years his capital had vanished. In 1959 he was involved in an horrific crash and suffered a fractured skull. He never really recovered from that and in 1965, aged sixty-two, he died after a heart attack.

A genius of his time, Walter Hammond was worshipped by the crowds and revered by his colleagues.

'A Genius of his Time', Walter Hammond.

1929 team. Back row, left to right: A.E. Dipper, C.J. Barnett, W.L. Neale, T.W.J. Goddard, R.A. Sinfield, E.J. Stephens, H. Smith. Front row: W.R. Hammond, C.W.L. Parker, B.H. Lyon (captain), L.P. Hedges, F.J. Seabrook.

With Bev Lyon as captain, Gloucestershire finished the season in fourth place in the Championship, their highest position since 1898. In fact, they had the chance of finishing first but were ousted from top spot when Nottinghamshire visited Bristol and won an exciting match by 6 runs. Though they returned to head the table, they suffered a one run defeat against Sussex at Cheltenham, but had they won these two narrowest of defeats Gloucestershire would have been champions. Tom Goddard returned after a season at the Lord's nets as an outstanding off-spinner, taking 154 wickets in the Championship at 15.97 runs each. In fact, Gloucestershire won fifteen of their twenty-eight matches compared to fourteen by Nottinghamshire, the eventual champions.

1930 team. Back row, left to right: E.J. Stephens, H. Smith, C.J. Barnett, T.W.J. Goddard, W.L. Neale, R.A. Sinfield. Front row: W.R. Hammond, C.W.L. Parker, B.H. Lyon (captain), W. Tunnicliffe (secretary), F.J. Seabrook, A.E. Dipper, L.P. Hedges.

Gloucestershire won fifteen of its twenty-eight Championship games, more than anyone else, but had to settle for runners-up spot to the eventual champions Lancashire, who only won ten of their games. Walter Hammond scored 1,168 runs with a top score of 199 and was well supported by captain Bev Lyon, who hit 115 and 101 not out against Essex and was selected as one of *Wisden's* Cricketers of the Year. Charlie Parker took 162 wickets at 11.90, including 9 for 44 against Warwickshire at Cheltenham and a hat-trick against Essex at Chelmsford. This was also a season in which D.N. Moore scored 206 against Oxford University in his first game for the County, and the summer in which the tied game against Australia took place.

ev Lyon (1921–47). Bev Lyon's approach to cricket and
ptaincy was a simple one – batting meant that the ball had to
e hit, and in bowling the ball had to hit the wicket. Each
ame was there to be won but, most of all, the game was there
o be enjoyed – by all! He had a cavalier approach to the game
nd was held in the greatest respect by all those who played
nder him. The County enjoyed greater success under his
spiring leadership than it had in the years before. In 1929,
s first year in charge, the County won fifteen matches and
eat the South Africans.

He was well known throughout the game for his adventurous
eclarations – often declaring behind his opponent's score if he
ought there was an opportunity for a victory. In a very short
ace of time Bev Lyon had changed Gloucestershire into a
ery exciting side to watch. He must certainly have had one of
e best cricketing brains for he could assess more accurately
an others what could be achieved.

A hard-hitting batsman and a brave fielder, taking the
ajority of his catches at either short-leg or in the slips, he
ill be remembered for the flair and imagination he brought
o the position of captain.

Billy Neale (1923–48). A member of the famous Berkeley Vale
farming and hunting family, Billy Neale learned his cricket at
Cirencester Grammar School, where he was a contemporary
of Walter Hammond. He first played for the County as an
amateur in 1923, not turning professional until six years later.
By 1927, though, Neale had become a regular and established
middle-order batsman and during this season hit the highest
score of his career, 145 not out against Hampshire at
Southampton. In Gloucestershire's next match against Essex at
the Fry's Ground, he scored exactly 100.

Whenever the ball turned, Billy Neale was in his element –
his upright stance and sound defence making him difficult to
dislodge. In 1937 he hit 121 and Walter Hammond 217 as they
put on 321 for the Gloucestershire fourth wicket – still a
County record. Though he occasionally bowled leg-spinners
'for fun in the nets', he found a length that summer in the
match against Somerset and took 6 for 9.

Billy Neale never criticised an umpire's decision. He played
at a time when there was a dividing line between Gentlemen
and Players. He could have played for the Gentlemen with
credit – for he was one of Nature's gentlemen.

Set of Ogden's cigarette cards – clockwise from top left, D.C. Robinson, W.R. Hammond, C.J. Barnett, T.W.J. Goddard.

Tom Goddard (1922–52). Tom Goddard began his cricketing career as a not too successful fast bowler. Despite his strong physique, his six seasons at Gloucestershire only brought him 153 wickets at a cost of over 34 runs each, including the hat-trick against Sussex at Eastbourne in 1924. Goddard left the County, accepting that he was a failure as a county cricketer, and joined the Lord's ground staff.

It was Bev Lyon who persuaded the Committee to re-engage him and in 1929, the first year of his second spell with the County, he took 184 wickets with his off-breaks that he had developed at Lord's. The following year he performed his second hat-trick and made his Test debut against Australia at Old Trafford. Goddard appeared in eight Tests for his country and in 1938–9 performed the hat-trick against South Africa at Johannesburg.

Tom Goddard was a big man, standing 6 ft 3 ins, with massive hands. He could spin the ball so much that on a helpful wicket he was almost unplayable. On sixteen occasions he took 100 wickets or more in a season, four times reaching 200 wickets. His most successful season was 1937 when he took 248 wickets. In the match against Worcestershire he took 6 for 68 in the first innings, but in the second took all 10 wickets for 113 runs. On seven occasions that season, he took 9 wickets in an innings and two years later achieved the magnificent feat of taking 17 wickets in a day against Kent at Bristol.

He finally retired in 1952 at the ripe old age of fifty-one, having taken 2,979 wickets in all matches at an average of 19.84 – only Rhodes, Freeman, Parker and J.T. Hearne having taken more.

Reg Sinfield (1924–39). After making a pair on his County Championship debut against Worcestershire at Cheltenham, Reg Sinfield went on to become one of the best all-rounders in the County's history. After batting in the lower order, his technique improved so much that he opened the innings, first with Dipper and later with Barnett. He scored more than 1,000 runs in a season on ten occasions with a best of 1,740 in 1935. His highest score also came this season when he made 209 not out against Glamorgan at Cardiff Arms Park.

On the bowling front he was used as first change, coming on after the new ball to do a containing job before the spinners came on. However, as Charlie Parker was coming to the end of his career, Sinfield began to take over the role as one of the main spinners. He took 100 wickets in a season four times with 161 at 19.14 each in 1936 his best.

He played in just one Test against the 1938 Australians, dismissing Don Bradman at Trent Bridge. He served the County as an all-rounder for fifteen years, scoring 15,561 runs and taking 1,165 wickets before becoming cricket coach at Clifton College.

Basil Allen (1932–51). Like most of the pre-war amateur captains who resumed control after the hostilities, Basil Allen was determined to maintain the old distinctions. In fact, Allen was the only amateur in 1947 who had sufficient leadership experience, and under his captaincy Gloucestershire continued to play positive attacking cricket. During the summer of 1947, a season in which Gloucestershire finished as runners-up in the County Championship, Allen hit the highest score of his career, 220 against Hampshire at Bournemouth.

Allen was also a superb fielder. During his career the new lbw law was introduced and he was able in his position of close in on the leg-side to snap up many chances. He held catches from the hottest of shots and in 1938 he made 42 catches, being worth his place in the side for his fielding alone. He continued as captain until 1950 and played a few games the following season before leaving the first-class game. The Clifton-born batsman gave the County great service both as a player and captain, and was President of the Club from 1978 to 1980.

Charlie Barnett (1927–48). First playing for Gloucestershire while still a sixteen-year-old pupil at Wycliff School, he served a long apprenticeship, always encouraged and supported by his excellent captain, Bev Lyon. It was 1930 before he passed the 1,000 run mark and 1933 before he hit his first century in the County Championship.

His straight driving in the arc between wide mid-on and extra cover was brilliant and his opening batting style often set the momentum of the innings. In 1933 Gloucestershire made 196 without loss before lunch in the match against Worcestershire, Barnett's contribution being 107. That season he scored over 2,000 runs including six hundreds, played for the Players and was chosen for one Test against the West Indies.

Perhaps his most dramatic innings was played at Bath in 1934. He had already hit eleven sixes when he was caught on the boundary going in for a twelfth that would have given him a double century! In 1936 he scored 2,107 runs and was selected as one of *Wisden*'s Five Cricketers of the Year. The following season he scored 2,489 runs including a career best of 232 against Lancashire. In 1938 he reached 98 in the penultimate over before lunch in the Trent Bridge Test against Australia; but Len Hutton played each ball defensively before Barnett hit the first ball after lunch for 4 to reach a deserved century.

Barnett played in twenty Tests and scored two centuries, both against Australia. A player with natural attacking instinct, he batted through an innings against Leicestershire in 1948, scoring 228 not out of Gloucestershire's total of 363. He was also a more than good enough bowler, taking 371 wickets for the County, though typically modest, he claimed that he only did it to take the shine off for the spinners!

Photo : Western Daily Press
Gloucestershire team v Australia 1930
R. G. Ford (12th man); B. S. Bloodworth (Scorer); A. E. Dipper
E. J. Stephens; C. C. Dacre; R. A. Sinfield; W. R. Hammond
W. L. Neale; C. J. Barnett; H. Smith
C. W. L. Parker; B. H. Lyon; F. J. Seabrook; T. W. Goddard

The Gloucestershire side that played in the historic tie with the Australians at Bristol in 1930.

The start of the Gloucestershire *vs* Australia match in August 1930 was held up for two hours because of early morning rain, but when play did get underway Vic Richardson the Australian captain asked Gloucestershire to bat. He appeared to have made a wise decision as they were all out for 72 just before the end of the day. The Australians did not find run-getting easy on the Monday but owing to Ponsford and Bradman they reached 157. With a lead of 85 on the first innings, the tourists seemed in an unassailable position but Hammond, with a magnificent 89, spearheaded a Gloucestershire fightback. However, once he had left, wickets fell quickly, the remaining 6 adding only 36 runs. Gloucestershire were all out for 202, leaving the Australians a seemingly simple task of scoring 118 to win. After forty-five minutes' play, the openers were still there having hit exactly half the number of runs required for victory. There then came an amazing transformation, for Parker who had seemingly been mastered suddenly had all the batsmen bewildered.

As the wickets began to tumble, the crowd sensed the possibility of a Gloucestershire victory, especially after Parker had bowled Bradman. The excitement reached fever pitch when, with the last pair at the wicket, just three runs were needed for victory. A boundary would have settled the issue, but two singles levelled the scores. The scores remained level on the two innings for twelve minutes while one ball and two consecutive maiden overs were bowled, with the Australian last pair together. They seemed content to wait for a winning run to come, but then Hornibrook, the Australian number ten, was beaten by Tom Goddard, and as the ball rapped him on the pads he was given out lbw.

George Emmett (1936–59). Born in Agra, India, the son of a soldier serving in the British Army, he started his cricketing career on the Lord's ground staff before playing Minor County cricket for Devon. After several successful seasons with Devon he began to qualify for Gloucestershire and made his debut in 1936 in a match against India at Cheltenham. Initially he was considered a replacement for Charlie Parker, but he soon set himself up as a fine attacking batsman. Unfortunately his progress was halted by the Second World War and so it wasn't until 1947 that he began to fulfil all that was expected of him. That season he hit hundreds in each innings of the match against Leicestershire at Grace Road, and in 1948 made his Test debut against the Australians. In 1949 he topped the 2,000 run mark for the first time and the following season hit the highest score of his career, 188 against Kent. In 1951 he once again topped 2,000 runs and hit hundreds in the match against Somerset at Bristol. Two years later he scored 2,115 runs, including a second innings century against the Australians. In 1954, in the match against Somerset at Taunton, he scored the season's fastest century, reaching three figures in eighty-four minutes.

    Captain of Gloucestershire from 1955 to 1958, George Emmett was a wonderful servant – a great team man, he was always prepared to vary his game to the needs of the team.

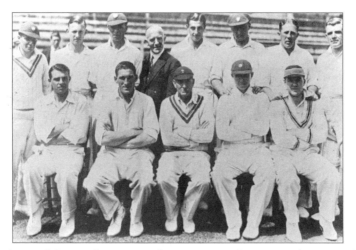

1932 team. Back row, left to right: E.J. Stephens, R.G. Ford, W.L. Neale, F.C. Burgess (scorer), J.A. Rogers, C.J. Barnett, C.C.R. Dacre, B.S. Bloodworth. Front row: G.W. Parker, T.W.J. Goddard, C.W.L. Parker, A.E. Dipper, B.O. Allen.

After finishing runners-up in the County Championship in 1931, Gloucestershire slipped to thirteenth as captain Bev Lyon was prevented by business commitments from playing in more than nine matches. Hammond who had the captaincy thrust upon him scored 2,528 runs at an average of 62 and hit six centuries, including an innings of 264 against Lancashire at Aigburth. This summer was Alf Dipper's last, and the County's debt to the Deerhurst-born batsman cannot be over-estimated.

1933 team. Back row, left to right: W.L. Neale, J.A. Rogers, P.I. Van der Gucht, D.A.C. Page, C.C.R. Dacre, E.J. Stephens. Front row: R.A. Sinfield, W.R. Hammond, B.H. Lyon (captain), C.W.L. Parker, T.W.J. Goddard.

The County moved up slightly in the Championship to tenth place, winning ten of its games. Bev Lyon only missed two games and there can be no doubt that his presence in the side contributed to the County's improvement. Hammond was again in superb form and in all matches scored 3,323 runs, breaking W.G. Grace's record for the highest number of runs in a season by a Gloucestershire player, which was 2,739 set by the Champion in 1871. Hammond averaged 65 in the Championship and scored eleven centuries in all matches, including 264 against the West Indies, 231 against Derbyshire and 206 against Leicestershire, when he and Bev Lyon added 336 for the second wicket. Charlie Barnett scored 2,161 runs at an average of 41.55, and Tom Goddard took 183 wickets at 17.41 runs apiece.

Jack Crapp (1936–56). Cornishman Jack Crapp made his debut against Oxford University in the opening match of 1936 and in his first season scored 1,052 runs, including a score of 168 against Sussex at Eastbourne. In his early days Crapp, a solidly built left-hander, was sometimes criticised for being reliable rather than spectacular!

He was thought of as in the Maurice Leyland mould but nobody could hit the ball harder when the occasion demanded. In 1938 he was being talked of as a potential England batsman but along came the war, and he had to wait another ten years before making his Test debut. After facing Lindwall and Miller in three Tests against the 1948 Australians, he toured South Africa the following winter where he played in the last four Tests, scoring 231 runs at 38.50. On this tour he scored hundreds against the Eastern Province and Orange Free State, but he never represented his country again.

For Gloucestershire Jack Crapp hit 1,000 runs or more in fourteen of the fifteen years in which he played county cricket, with a best of 2,014 in 1949. He was awarded a benefit against Lancashire in 1951 and two years later went down in history as Gloucestershire's first professional captain. The following season of 1954 was probably the County's worst season for twenty years and was the only one in which Crapp didn't reach 1,000 runs. He was suffering from eczema on his hands and was pleased to hand over the role to George Emmett.

When he retired in 1956 he had scored 23,615 runs including thirty-eight centuries. The following year he joined the first-class umpire's list, standing for twenty-one years, including four Tests in the mid-1960s.

George Lambert (1938–57). His name appeared on the score sheet for the first time in 1938 with other names like Jack Crapp, George Emmett and Colin Scott, all of whom were to make their mark after the war. A tall, muscular bowler, his fast-medium in-swing brought him 908 wickets for the County as he turned in sustained spells of pace bowling. Lambert had such a lovely bowling action that boys of that era tried to copy it.

As a batsman he would usually go in at number six, seven or eight. He could certainly bat soundly, although he only had one century to his name. He once helped Basil Allen in a partnership of 148 against Sussex at Eastbourne, Lambert's bold strikes enabling him to collect 68 quick-fire runs and Gloucestershire to win the match by an innings and 26 runs.

A popular cricketer, he was awarded a well-deserved benefit match, choosing the visit of Sussex to the County Ground in 1955. Two years later he played his last game for the County, having taken almost 1,000 wickets and scored over 6,000 runs – a great contribution from this most modest of players.

Charlie Dacre (1928–36). Charlie Dacre was born in New Zealand where he played first-class cricket before he'd reached the age of sixteen. After scoring 45 and 58 for a representative New Zealand side against Archie MacLaren's MCC team in 1923, he was named as vice-captain of the first New Zealand side to tour England. Though he hit two centuries in his first two matches, it was at Gloucestershire's expense that Dacre gave one of his best displays as he hit 64 in less than half-an-hour, reaching his half-century in fifteen minutes.

At the end of the tour, he approached Gloucestershire with a view to playing for them, as it was his father's native county. The regulations of the period, however, required Dacre to qualify by residence until 1930. After qualifying, he hit his very first ball in County Championship cricket on to the pavilion roof for six, and in that season hit 1,381 runs, including his highest score of 223 not out against Worcestershire at New Road.

In 1933 Bev Lyon tried Dacre as an opening batsman and he responded by scoring 119 and 128 not out in the match at Worcester. A powerful hitter and a superb fielder in the deep, he played a great part in the County's revival.

1936 team. Back row, left to right: E.J. Stephens, V. Hopkins, R.W. Haynes, L.M. Cranfield, J.F. Crapp, C.I. Monks, B.S. Bloodworth (scorer). Front row: W.K. Neale, R.A. Sinfield, W.R. Hammond, D.A.C. Page (captain), T.W.J. Goddard, C.J. Barnett, C.C.R. Dacre.

After a disappointing first season as captain in 1935 when the County finished fifteenth, Dallas Page began to gain respect from both his team-mates and opponents and led the side to fourth in the table. Tragically, the Gloucestershire captain was killed in a car crash immediately after the last match of the season against Nottinghamshire.

The batting was solid enough with both Charlie Barnett and Walter Hammond scoring 2,107 runs and the latter batsman 1,281 runs in August alone. Jack Crapp scored 1,052 runs in what was his first full season. On the bowling front, Tom Goddard took 150 wickets and Reg Sinfield 146.

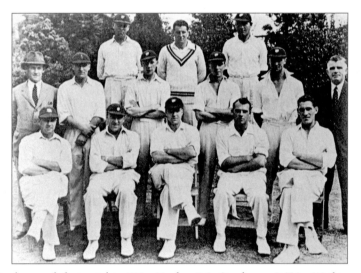

1937 team. Back row, left to right: W.L. Neale, E.J. Stephens, B.T.L. Watkins. Middle row: -?-, R.A. Sinfield, C.J. Barnett, L.M. Cranfield, R.W. Haynes, B.S. Bloodworth (scorer). Front row: W.R. Hammond, B.H. Lyon, B.O. Allen (captain), G.W. Parker, T.W.J. Goddard.

The new County captain was Basil Allen and he led the club to fourth again. The batting was always reliable with Walter Hammond scoring over 3,000 runs for the second time and Charlie Barnett 2,489 runs. Despite the bowling resting entirely on Sinfield and Goddard, it was so successful that fifteen of the thirty matches were won.

Tom Goddard took 248 wickets including 10 for 113 in the match against Worcestershire and Sinfield, who took 129 wickets, did the double for the second time in his career. The season also saw, for the first time since 1883, three Gloucestershire players – Hammond, Barnett and Goddard – play in the same Test match against New Zealand at Old Trafford.

ndy Wilson (1936–55). Having previously been a member of
he Lord's ground staff, Andy Wilson celebrated his first
ummer in the Gloucestershire side by hitting 130 against
Middlesex, the county of his birth, at Lord's while wearing his
Middlesex Second XI cap!

A very reliable wicket-keeper, his career spanned the Second
World War, and after scoring 1,000 runs for the second time in
946 including a century on his first appearance as an opening
atsman in the match against Oxford University, he scored
,294 runs in 1947, his best season in terms of runs scored.

It is said that the hallmark of a good wicket-keeper is that he
hould be unobtrusive – Andy Wilson was certainly that. In
Gloucestershire's match against Essex in 1947, Ray Smith
wept a delivery from Sam Cook on the leg-side. The fieldsmen
vere all in front of the bat, so off set Andy, chasing the ball all
he way down to long leg. He caught it a yard or so from the
oundary rope and threw the ball – typical of the man who
laimed 585 victims (416 caught and 169 stumped) during his
Gloucestershire career.

Colin Scott (1938–54). Though fair-haired fast bowler Colin
Scott's early performances were modest, H.E. Roslyn writing
in *Wisden* was not deceived. He wrote: 'Although Scott's
record was not impressive, his fine action, height and youth
suggested he would do well in the near future.' Hailing from
W.G. Grace's village of Downend, Scott's outswing bowling
paid dividends in 1939, his second season in the
Gloucestershire side, when he took 113 wickets in the
Championship at 22 runs each.

Scott was only twenty when the Second World War broke
out, but despite missing six seasons of county cricket much
was expected of him. Sadly his pre-war promise was unfulfilled
and in 1949 he attempted to convert to off-spin as Tom
Goddard had done. However, it was not until 1952 when he
returned to swing bowling, by then at a more medium pace,
that he was again successful, taking 101 wickets at 25 runs
apiece. He played his last game for the County in 1954, having
taken 531 wickets at 31.57 runs each, and a best performance
of 8 for 90 against Surrey.

1938 team. Back row, left to right: B.S. Bloodworth (scorer), G.M. Emmett, J.F. Crapp, R.W. Haynes, L.M. Cranfield, A.E. Wilson. Front row: R.A. Sinfield, T.W.J. Goddard, W.R. Hammond, B.O. Allen (captain), E.D.R. Eager, C.J. Barnett, W.L. Neale.

The County's drop to tenth position this season was accounted for by Tom Goddard's tendency to push the ball through too quickly and therefore lose his line and length. His 107 wickets cost just under 23 runs apiece, and with Sinfield and Emmett proving expensive, the County were pleased to unearth a new fast bowler in Colin Scott.

Turning amateur, Walter Hammond captained England in four Test matches, and with Charlie Barnett hitting 99 not out before lunch in the Trent Bridge Test, the County's Test players gave good accounts of themselves. In the Championship, seven Gloucestershire batsmen exceeded 1,000 runs for the season – Hammond, Barnett, Crapp, Allen, Neale, Wilson and Emmett.

1939 team. Back row, left to right: B.S. Bloodworth (scorer), V. Hopkins, C.J. Scott, Col. H.A. Hanson (secretary), G.E.E. Lambert, J.F. Crapp, A.O.H. Mills. Front row: G.M. Emmett, C.J. Barnett, R.A. Sinfield, W.R. Hammond (captain), T.W.J. Goddard, W.L. Neale, A.E. Wilson.

Walter Hammond took over the Gloucestershire captaincy and led the side to third position in the Championship as they won eighteen and lost seven of their games. Though Yorkshire carried off the title, the County had the satisfaction of completing the double over them. Gloucestershire had been the last side to achieve the feat, five years earlier.

Tom Goddard was back to his best form, taking 181 wickets in the Championship at 14.66 each, and with a new pair of opening bowlers in Colin Scott and George Lambert the County's attack was quite strong. Gloucestershire were a powerful side in 1939 and one wonders how they might have developed if six seasons hadn't been lost to the Second World War.

CHAPTER FOUR

1946–97

Because the wickets at Bristol and Cheltenham tend to discourage fast bowlers and encourage the tweakers, Gloucestershire's tradition is one of fine spinners. Tom Goddard was still going strong after the war and in 1947, when Gloucestershire finished runners-up in the Championship, twenty points adrift of Middlesex, he took 206 wickets with his off-breaks and Sam Cook 120 with his left-arm spin. Cook, in fact, was to bowl well for two decades, but apart from Colin Scott, George Lambert and Ken Graveney, who took all 10 wickets for 66 in 1949, there was little support until the advent of off-spinner 'Bomber' Wells and two of the same type who went on to represent England, John Mortimore and David Allen.

In the years immediately following the war, the Gloucestershire batting was very attractive. Walter Hammond scored six centuries in his first sixteen innings but his career was virtually over, as was Charlie Barnett's. George Emmett was still charming the West Country crowds with his attractive strokeplay, but in 1948 a young batsman by the name of Tom Graveney stepped into Hammond's shoes. He had every shot, including a very good hook for a tall player, and it was a severe blow to the County when he decided to leave after losing the captaincy to Tom Pugh in 1960. Other members of a strong Gloucestershire batting side in the 1950s were Arthur Milton, Jack Crapp and Martin Young, while Ron Nicholls made at least some of the runs Graveney would have gone on making had he not gone to Worcestershire.

Following Tom Graveney's departure, Ken Graveney, Arthur Milton and John Mortimore tried their hands at captaincy, but in 1964 and 1967 Gloucestershire finished bottom of the Championship, and seldom threatened to win a limited-over title.

In 1965 Gloucestershire had acquired the services of South African Mike Procter, who in the 1970s was probably the finest all-rounder in English cricket. A turning point in the County's fortunes came in 1968 with the arrival of David Green, a hard-hitting opening batsman from Lancashire and the appointment of the County's good opening bowler and capable batsman Tony Brown as captain. He remained so until 1976 when he became secretary, then handed over as captain to Procter.

In the 1970s Gloucestershire were a force to be reckoned with in the Championship, finishing third three times, and had two glorious occasions, which are expanded upon later in the book, winning the Gillette Cup under Brown in 1973 and the Benson and Hedges Cup under Procter in 1977.

Two Pakistani Test players, Sadiq Mohammed and Zaheer Abbas, shared Brown's success in 1973. The better of the two was Zaheer, a superb wristy batsman who scored a century and a double century in the same match for Gloucestershire three times in 1976 and 1977. In that glorious summer of 1976 he scored 2,554 runs at 75.11. Sadiq was the youngest of the famous Mohammed brotherhood, and though he was never perhaps as good a player as Mushtaq or Hanif he did hit four consecutive Championship hundreds in 1976.

Other useful members of that Gloucestershire side in 1973 were David Shepherd, Roger Knight, Andy Stovold and David Graveney.

Later in the 1970s Mike Procter's team depended so much upon his personal inspiration – he had three Championship hat-tricks to his credit and another in the Benson and Hedges Cup – that it became known as 'Proctershire'.

In the years that followed, Gloucestershire's record in both the Championship and the one-day game was disappointing, but after finishing third in the Championship in 1985 the County went one better the following summer.

Finishing in second place behind Essex, who had ten wins to Gloucestershire's nine, the County's performance was a tribute to David Graveney's leadership qualities and to the excellent spirit of the side. It was a remarkable achievement considering that Curran had to undergo a shoulder operation, Bill Athey missed eleven matches through England calls and Davison was unable to play owing to registration difficulties caused by the refusal of the Home Office to grant him British citizenship. The County's present captain, Mark Alleyne, scored 116 not out against Sussex, to become at eighteen, the youngest player in the County's history to make a century. The bowling depended heavily on Courtney Walsh, and he responded magnificently with 118 wickets in the Championship at 18.17 runs apiece.

Unfortunately, weather affected Gloucestershire's chances of lifting the title when it forced them to chase highly improbable targets in matches involving forfeitures and contrived finishes.

Since that successful summer, twelve years ago, the County have had mixed fortunes with bests of sixth in the Championship in 1995, runners-up in the Sunday League in 1988 and, after reaching the semi-final of the Nat West Trophy in 1987, never going further than the quarter-final in either the Nat West or Benson and Hedges Cup in that period.

1946 team. Back row, left to right: C. Cook, W.L. Neale, G.E.E. Lambert, C.J. Scott, B.S. Bloodworth (scorer), A.G.S. Wilcox, V. Hopkins, L.M. Cranfield. Front row: C.J. Barnett, B.O. Allen, W.R. Hammond (captain), T.W.J. Goddard, A.E. Wilson.

Despite finishing fifth in the first Championship after the hostilities, it was regarded as something of a disappointment. Walter Hammond was still captain and though he only batted in sixteen Championship innings because of his Test calls, he still scored 1,404 runs at an average of 108.00. Only Tom Goddard and Sam Cook found success with the ball. Though he was now forty-five, Goddard took 150 Championship wickets at less than 18 runs each and Cook in his first full season took 113 Championship wickets at a similar cost. Cook also took a wicket with the first ball of the first game he played after the war in the match against Oxford University.

1947 team. Back row, left to right: J.F. Crapp, C. Cook, G.E.E. Lambert, C.J. Scott, A.G.S. Wilcox, G.M. Emmett, L.M. Cranfield, A.E. Wilson. Front row: C.J. Barnett, T.W.J. Goddard, Lt-Col. H.A. Hanson (secretary), B.O. Allen (captain), B.S. Bloodworth (scorer), W.L. Neale.

In one of the closest races in the County Championship for years, Gloucestershire, who won eighteen of their matches under captain Basil Allen, finished runners-up to Middlesex. Though Jack Crapp made almost 2,000 runs and Allen himself well over 1,500, including a career best of 220 against Hampshire at Bournemouth, it was the bowlers who almost won the title for the County.

Tom Goddard took 238 wickets and performed the hat-trick against Glamorgan and Somerset, where in the cider county's second innings he took 5 for 4 in seven balls. Sam Cook took 9 for 42 against Yorkshire and played in his only Test match. The title was decided in mid-August when Middlesex visited Cheltenham and won by 68 runs inside two days.

Sam Cook (1946–64). After serving in the RAF and playing cricket in Rhodesia, Sam Cook joined the County on a recommendation from A.P.F. Singleton who captained the RAF side in Bulawayo. Selected for the opening game of the 1946 season against Oxford University, he took a wicket with his first ball and at the end of the season had taken 133 wickets, 113 in the Championship at 18.05 runs each.

In his second season he captured 138 wickets including a career best 9 for 42 against Yorkshire at Bristol. Cook was always admired by the older county players because he had the important asset of being able to maintain an immaculate length. In normal seasons he had no difficulty in taking over 100 wickets but 1956 was without doubt his best year, when he took 149 wickets at a cost of only 14.16 runs apiece.

In 1962 Sam Cook topped the national averages, although he only took 58 wickets. In all first-class matches he took 1,768 wickets at an average of 20.26 runs each. He retired in 1964 and joined the umpire's list the following season.

Arthur Milton (1948–74). A double international, Arthur Milton played soccer for England against Austria in 1951 and appeared in six Test matches, the first against New Zealand in 1958. During his two years' National Service Milton played twice for Gloucestershire, his performances being so good that the County offered him a contract when he had completed his army training. Milton's ability was such that he was awarded his county cap in 1949.

On the football front he made seventy-five league appearances for First Division Arsenal before joining his home-town club Bristol City, whom he helped to win the Third Division championship before ending his football career at the age of twenty-seven.

He then turned to cricket full time. A batsman with the correct technique for dealing with any type of bowling, he topped the 1,000 run mark for Gloucestershire for sixteen seasons. He became the first Gloucestershire player to score 100 on his Test debut since W.G. Grace, and in that game against New Zealand he became the first England cricketer to be on the field throughout a Test match as the Kiwis lost inside three days.

One of the game's finest all-round fielders, he held 719 catches and played more innings for the County than any other player. His contribution to Gloucestershire cricket was immense.

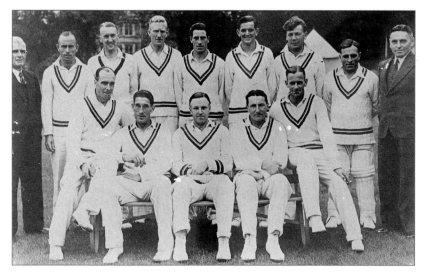

1948 team. Back row, left to right: B.S. Bloodworth (scorer), C. Cook, A.G.S. Wilcox, C.J. Scott, G.E.E. Lambert, T.W. Graveney, L.M. Cranfield, A.E. Wilson, R. Sowden (masseur). Front row: J.F. Crapp, T.W.J. Goddard, B.O. Allen (captain), C.J. Barnett, G.M. Emmett.

That the County slipped to eighth in the Championship this season was a result of a more placid Bristol wicket. When the Australians played there they totalled 774 for 7 with Arthur Morris making 290. The spin bowlers Goddard and Cook took fewer wickets at greater cost but nine matches were won against eight defeats. One of the County's victories was against Yorkshire at Bristol, where, after Gloucestershire had struggled to avoid the follow-on, they were set 389 for victory in a little under four hours. Barnett and Emmett added 226 in two hours for the first wicket, and with Barnett in his last season, scoring 141, the target was reached with forty-five minutes to spare.

1949 team. Back row, left to right: C.A. Milton, J.R.K. Graveney, G.E.E. Lambert, T.W. Graveney, A.G.S. Wilcox, L.M. Cranfield, A.E. Wilson, B.S. Bloodworth (scorer). Front row: J.F. Crapp, T.W.J. Goddard, B.O. Allen (captain), G.M. Emmett, C. Cook.

Seventh position this summer was a satisfactory outcome for a Gloucestershire side still lacking the all-round bowling strength to challenge the leading counties. Tom Goddard was still Gloucestershire's leading bowler with 152 wickets in the Championship at 18.60, though swing bowler Ken Graveney forced his way into the side, and in the match against Derbyshire at Chesterfield he took all 10 wickets for 66 runs.

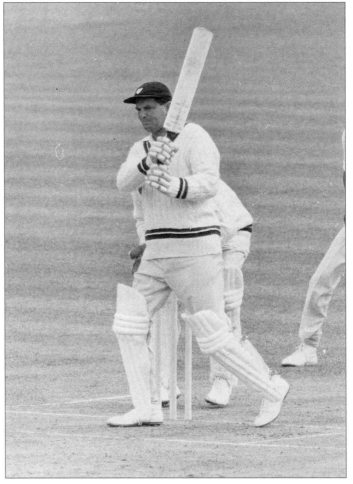

Tom Graveney (1948–60). Northumberland-born Tom Graveney had a natural talent for the game and this, together with a recommendation from his elder brother Ken (already on the Gloucestershire staff), brought him to Bristol. He got a duck on his first-class debut and, after a series of low scores, he was dropped. Eventually, later that season, his chance came again and after scoring 40 on a turning wicket he proceeded to hit over 700 runs in the month of August.

In 1951 Graveney scored 2,291 runs, including innings of 103 and 105 not out against Northamptonshire at Bristol. In 1951–2 he was England's number three in the tour of India, Pakistan and Ceylon and scored 1,393 runs including six centuries. The following summer his aggregate of runs was 2,066 and he was selected as one of *Wisden*'s Cricketers of the Year. In 1954 Graveney hit 222 against Derbyshire at Chesterfield; it was his highest score for Gloucestershire. In 1953–4 he represented the MCC in their fixture against British Guyana at Georgetown. He scored 231 as he and Willie Watson added 402 for the fourth wicket – still a record for any English touring team.

In 1956 he topped the County's averages, scoring 2,397 runs and in the match against Essex produced a remarkable achievement. He scored more than half his side's total in both innings of that match: 100 out of 153 and then 67 out of 107. Also that season he scored a magnificent 200 out of his side's total of 298. Although he appeared in seventy-nine Tests, it wasn't until 1957 that he established himself as a regular, after hitting 258 against the West Indies at Trent Bridge and later following it with 164 at The Oval.

He played for Gloucestershire for twelve years, being their captain for the last two, and in 1959 led the side to runners-up in the Championship. After leaving Gloucestershire in 1960, he joined Worcestershire and helped them win the Championship in 1964 and 1965. In 1968 he received the OBE for his services to cricket.

A set of Turf cigarette cards.

1950 team. Back row, left to right: C. Cook, G.E.E. Lambert, T.W. Graveney, L.M. Cranfield, J.R.K. Graveney, C.A. Milton, D.M. Young. Front row: A.E. Wilson, T.W.J. Goddard, G.W. Parker, B.O. Allen (captain), Lt-Col. H.A. Hanson (secretary), Sir D. Bailey, G.M. Emmett.

In a wet summer in which rain interfered with most of the County's home games, Gloucestershire again finished seventh with six wins against seven defeats. It was Basil Allen's final season of captaincy, and in the six seasons he was officially in charge the County's worst position was tenth in 1938 and their best was second in 1947; the others were fourth, seventh twice and eighth. Goddard and Cook each took just under 140 wickets and George Lambert had his best season with 95 wickets, though they were slightly expensive at 27 runs each. On the batting front, George Emmett was the top scorer in the Championship with 1,737 runs, while Martin Young established himself as Emmett's opening partner.

1951 team. Back row, left to right: C.A. Milton, B.D. Wells, C. Cook, J.B. Mortimore, C.J. Scott, T.W. Graveney, G.E.E. Lambert. Front row: A.E. Wilson, J.F. Crapp, Sir D. Bailey (captain), B.O. Allen, G.M. Emmett.

Basil Allen's successor as captain was Sir Derrick Bailey DFC, the son of the South African industrialist Sir Abe Bailey. His first season in charge saw the County slip from seventh position in the table to twelfth. The reasons for this were that no bowler took 100 wickets, the first time the feat had not been achieved since 1902. However, the batting was solid with Emmett scoring 2,019 runs, including 110 and 102 not out against Somerset. Tom Graveney also scored hundreds in the match against Northamptonshire and in all matches scored 2,291 runs, earning himself a Test debut against South Africa at Old Trafford.

rtin Young (1949–64). Martin Young was the link between
 amateur and the first-class career cricketer. Having
ended Wellingborough School, he certainly had the
hnique of a public school batsman to which he added the
sistency and determination of a professional.
Iis first senior games were spent representing
rcestershire but it wasn't too long before he joined
oucestershire. In 1950, his first full season for the County,
made 135 against his former county at New Road, the first
his forty first-class centuries. In 1955 he had his most
cessful season since he made his debut, scoring 2,016 runs.
 best performance came in the match against
rthamptonshire at Kettering when he scored 121 and 117
 out. Four years later, Young passed the 2,000 run mark
in, scoring 2,090 runs. In 1962 he and Ron Nicholls put on
5 for the first wicket in the match against Oxford
iversity – Young's share was 198. In 1963 he took 127 off
 West Indian attack that included Hall and Griffith, leaving
ir captain Frank Worrell wondering why 'Youngie' wasn't
he England side. The scorer of 23,400 runs for
oucestershire, he later became a recognised sports
adcaster in South Africa.

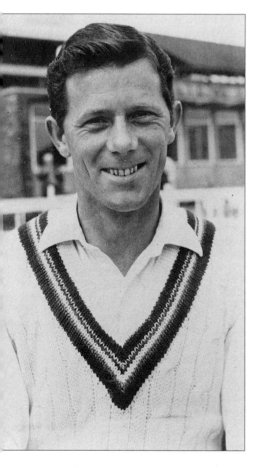

Ron Nicholls (1951–75). George Emmett was a good
influence on Ron Nicholls' formative years as his cricket
developed in the Etceteras alongside other Gloucestershire
players such as David Allen, Tony Brown and John Mortimore.
In 1961 Arthur Milton moved down the order and he became
the established No.1 batsman. He made 1,800 runs that
season, including 107 on the Stroud wicket – one of only four
centuries in fifty-one innings between 1956 and 1963 – a
remarkable achievement on a wicket that made life very
difficult for most batsmen. In 1962 he scored 2,059 runs with
a career best of 217 against Oxford University as he and
Martin Young shared a record first wicket stand of 395.

Cricket was always his first love, but while on National
Service he took up goalkeeping and played for both Bristol
clubs and Cardiff City before hanging up his boots in 1966.
That summer was Nicholls' benefit year, and he hit a hundred
before lunch in the Gillette Cup match against Berkshire.

While he occasionally bowled spinners, it was for his
graceful and stylish batting that he is remembered by cricket
lovers up and down the country, not just in Gloucestershire.
His 23,606 runs for the County provide ample testimony to
his established position over the years.

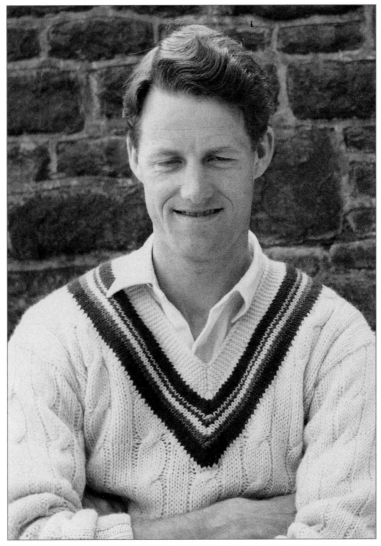

John Mortimore (1950–75). The retirement of Tom Goddard, forced on him by pneumonia, allowed John Mortimore the chance to make his mark with the County. In his first full season, he took 48 wickets before he left for National Service. When he returned to Gloucestershire in the summer of 1954 he was awarded his county cap.

From finishing his National Service until 1968 Mortimore used to spend his winters with Rediffusion, his job being to negotiate with landowners and householders for the right of way across their property for the installation of the wiring system. However, in 1958 he was flown out to Australia to reinforce the England side and, after playing in a number of State games, made his Test debut at Melbourne, before playing in all the games on the New Zealand leg of the tour.

The value of this tour was shown the following summer when he achieved the first double for the County since Reg Sinfield in 1937, scoring 1,060 runs and capturing 113 wickets with a best of 8 for 59 against Oxford University. He completed the double again in seasons 1962 and 1963 and in this latter season hit his maiden first-class century, 149 against Nottinghamshire. In 1965 he succeeded Ken Graveney as Gloucestershire captain, but gave up the position after three seasons in charge.

Mortimore's high elegant action graced Gloucestershire cricket for a quarter of a century, his 14,918 runs and 1,696 wickets being an outstanding achievement for this much-respected cricketer.

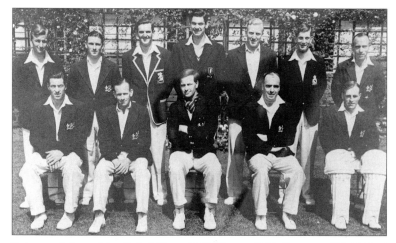

1952 team. Back row, left to right: C.A. Milton, D.M. Young, T.W. Graveney, F.P. McHugh, C.J. Scott, G.G.M. Wiltshire, C. Cook. Front row: G.E.E. Lambert, G.M. Emmett, Sir D. Bailey (captain), J.F. Crapp, A.E. Wilson.

This summer saw better performances from both batsmen and bowlers and resulted in the County moving up to ninth in the Championship. George Lambert, Sam Cook and Colin Scott all exceeded 100 wickets, while Young, Crapp, Emmett, Graveney and Milton all passed 1,000 runs, with the latter batsman heading the averages. Though only seven matches were won, rain almost certainly robbed the County of a further three wins. The most obvious of these being in the match against Somerset. After the cider county had followed-on, Gloucestershire were left to make 48 runs for victory in fifty minutes. Rain then restricted play to two spells of eight minutes in which five overs were bowled, and Gloucestershire 38 for 1!

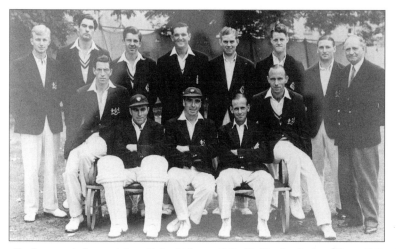

1953 team. Back row, left to right: C.A. Milton, F.P. McHugh, D.A. Allen, T.W. Graveney, J.V.C. Griffiths, J.B. Mortimore, D.M. Young, A.E. Crew (scorer). Front row: G.E.E. Lambert, A.E. Wilson, J.F. Crapp (captain), G.M. Emmett, C. Cook.

Appointing their first professional captain in Jack Crapp, Gloucestershire finished joint sixth in the Championship, having won eleven matches. They might have won even more, but from the middle of July the County embarked on a dreadful run which saw them lose seven of their next eight matches and drop from third into the bottom half of the table.

In a season which was generally considered to have favoured the bowler, Gloucestershire's did not do very well. George Emmett exceeded 2,000 runs in all games for the third time, but with Tom Graveney on Test duty and Arthur Milton selected as twelfth man on a number of occasions, the side suffered from their absence.

'Bomber' Wells (1951–9). 'Bomber' Wells as he was calle
after the boxer Bombardier Billy Wells, made his county
debut in 1951 in a match against Sussex in which he took 6
for 47. At the end of that season he went to do his two yea
National Service, and after he was released from Her
Majesty's Forces he immediately signed professional forms
for Gloucestershire. He never took too much out of himse
Sometimes he would shorten his run-up and his quick arm
action surprised many a batsman who had his stumps
uprooted while still admiring his stance!

There are many tales concerning 'Bomber'. He had just
bowled, the batsman played the ball into the covers and se
off for a run as did his partner. When the ball was returne
to 'Bomber' at the bowling end, both batsmen were in mi
wicket. He had ample time to remove the bails but hesitate
and then threw the ball to the far end and knocked out two
stumps. George Emmett couldn't believe his eyes. 'What'
going on, Bomber?' he inquired. 'Well, this bloke can't ba
it's the other . . . we wanted out' was Bomber's reply! A te
class spinner, he took 544 wickets for Gloucestershire befo
leaving to join Nottinghamshire.

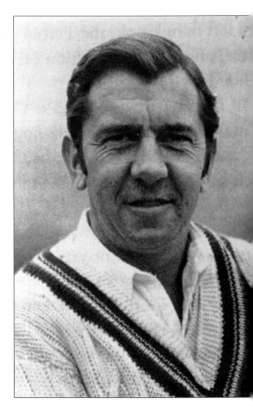

David Allen (1953–72). In one of his first games for
Gloucestershire in 1953, he helped defeat the previous season's
County Champions Surrey by taking 6 for 13 with just two balls
to go. He then did his National Service, but on returning to
first-class cricket found it difficult to win a place as Mortimore
and Wells were the County's established spinners. A few
months later, however, 'Bomber' Wells joined Nottinghamshire
and Allen started the 1959 season in the first team both to
improve the batting and maintain the high standard of off-spin
bowling. He ended the summer second only to Lancashire's
Brian Statham in the national bowling averages with 84 wickets
at 15.73 runs each.

He was included in the MCC team to tour the West Indies at
the end of the season, and with his very first touch of the ball in
the opening Test in Barbados ran out McMorris. He went on to
play thirty-nine times for England, taking 122 wickets. In 1960
he was voted Young Cricketer of the Year, and in 1961 became
the third Gloucestershire player to complete the double when
he scored 1,001 runs and took 124 wickets.

1954 team. Back row, left to right: E. Mains, B.D. Wells, J.B. Mortimore, R.B. Nicholls, A.B. Crew (scorer), F.P. McHugh, J.V.C. Griffiths, D.M. Young. Front row: G.E.E. Lambert, A.E. Wilson, J.F. Crapp (captain), G.M. Emmett, C. Cook.

In a very wet summer, Gloucestershire could only manage five victories and dropped to thirteenth in the Championship, though to be fair the matches against Lancashire and Leicestershire were abandoned without a ball being bowled. Tom Graveney scored 1,626 runs for an average of 73.90 in the Championship. He was well supported by Milton and Emmett, but Jack Crapp found his form badly affected by the cares of captaincy, and at the end of the season he handed over the reins to George Emmett.

1955 team. Back row, left to right: B.D. Wells, D.M. Young, J.V.C. Griffiths, W. Knightly-Smith, F.P. McHugh, J.B. Mortimore, G.G.M. Wiltshire, P. Rochford, T.W. Graveney, C.A. Milton. Front row: G.E.E. Lambert, Lt-Col. H.A. Hanson (secretary), G.M. Emmett (captain), J.F. Crapp.

In the first of George Emmett's four seasons as captain, the County only climbed one position to twelfth. It was a season of individual performances, for the team lacked consistency and often allowed a game to slip away from them after getting into a good position. Emmett dropped down the order, allowing Young and Milton to open the batting. The former scored over 2,000 runs for the first time and scored 121 and 117 not out in the match against Northamptonshire at Kettering. It was George Lambert's benefit year, and he responded by taking 77 wickets and hitting 100 not out against Worcestershire, his only first-class century.

Tony Brown (1953–76). Like many cricketers, Tony Brown joined his County as a batsman because as a schoolboy he had only bowled occasionally. After three seasons with Gloucestershire he was asked to bowl, and in 1957 was played primarily as a fast-medium seamer, bowling at a lively pace from a 10-yard run. He was awarded his county cap that summer by captain George Emmett who uttered the words: 'This is not for what you have done for Gloucestershire, but for what I know you will do in the future.' As it turned out, Emmett was a very shrewd judge. In 1959 Brown succeeded for the first time in passing 100 wickets in a season, including 7 for 11 against Yorkshire as the champions were shot out for 35!

In 1962 he captured more than 100 wickets for the second time and then the following year achieved his best figures with the ball, 8 for 80 against Essex at Leyton. He backed up his batting and bowling by his brilliant fielding in most positions. He ensured a place in *Wisden* when he held seven catches in an innings against Nottinghamshire at Trent Bridge, equalling Micky Stewart's world record. In his benefit year of 1969 he took over the captaincy and added great drive and confidence to the position, as the County finished second and third under his leadership. In 1971 he hit 116 against Somerset, his highest score for the County and at the end of the season he became the Assistant Secretary of the County Club. In 1973 he performed the hat-trick against Glamorgan at Swansea and that year captained the County to success in the final of the Gillette Cup, where he won the man of the match award after his innings of 77 not out. Retiring in 1976, Tony Brown was an exciting and genuine all-rounder, having made 12,684 runs, taken 1,223 wickets and held 489 catches.

1956 team. Back row, left to right: H.R. White (masseur), C.A. Milton, P. Rochford, B.D. Wells, J.V.C. Griffiths, J.B. Mortimore, G.J. Lake, R.B. Nicholls, D.M. Young. Front row: C. Cook, G.E.E. Lambert, G.M. Emmett (captain), Lt-Col. H.A. Hanson (secretary), J.F. Crapp, T.W. Graveney.

In its best season since 1947, the County finished third in the Championship, only four points adrift of runners-up Lancashire. It was a wet summer but the batsmen still managed to score runs. Tom Graveney, who was called on for only two Tests of the Ashes series, topped the batting averages with 1,787 runs at 52.20. His best knock was an innings of 200 out of a total of 298 against Glamorgan at Newport. However, it was chiefly a bowler's year with Sam Cook taking 139 Championship wickets at 14.39 each and 'Bomber' Wells 112 at 18.50 each.

1957 team. Back row, left to right: H.C.W. White (masseur), D.R. Smith, C.A. Milton, D. Carpenter, B.D. Wells, A.S. Brown, J.B. Mortimore, R.B. Nicholls, D.G. Hawkins, D.M. Young, B.S. Bloodworth (scorer). Front row: T.W. Graveney, Sir A.W. Grant (chairman), G.M. Emmett (captain), H. Thomas (secretary), C. Cook.

After the success of the previous season, hopes were high but despite a mid-season run of victories, the County slid down ten places to thirteenth. Jack Crapp had become an umpire and Arthur Milton was injured and didn't play until July, but Tom Graveney who only played in nineteen Championship games was in splendid form, hitting six centuries and averaging almost 50. George Emmett struggled in the early Championship matches, but in the match against the West Indians he hit 91 out of 111 in sixty-seven minutes before hitting a brilliant 170 in three hours in the match against Glamorgan. On the bowling front, David Smith in his first full season was given the new ball and responded with 94 wickets in the Championship, 106 in all matches.

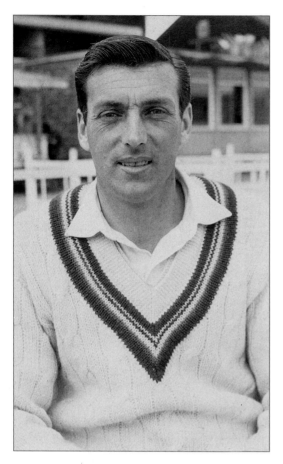

David Smith (1956–70). An England Youth international footballer, David Smith played a handful of games for Bristol City before joining Third Division Millwall, where his career ended at the end of the 1959–60 season. He had made his debut for Gloucestershire in 1956 although it was the following summer before he played on a regular basis. His firs full season in 1957 brought him 106 wickets, as his whippy action allowed him full control over his movement off the pitch, pace and swing. In 1959 he took 110 wickets in the County Championship and was being talked of as a possible England candidate. In 1960 Smith captured 143 first-class wickets and was chosen to tour New Zealand with the Englan 'B' team the following winter. After the summer of 1961 in which his performances almost won him a place in the Ashes series, he was chosen to tour India the following winter. On this trip he played in all five Tests, taking 6 wickets on pitches that were decidedly unfriendly.

David Smith was a cricketer's cricketer. His 1,159 wickets i his Gloucestershire career provided ample testimony to the fact that he was one of the most effective strike bowlers in the County's history.

Barry Meyer (1957–71). Barry Meyer gave long and reliable service to Gloucestershire County Cricket Club, yet he never expected to become a county cricketer and still less a wicket-keeper. He had captained his school team in Bournemouth but had played as a quick bowler who could score runs. Yet his first love at this time was soccer, and after playing in a trial he joined Bristol Rovers, making his Football League debut as an eighteen-year-old. He scored 60 goals in 139 League games for Rovers before later playing for Plymouth Argyle, Newport County and Bristol City. During the summer months he went along to the County Ground to help with odd jobs and get the occasional game for the ground staff side. He joined the ground staff in 1955 but played his first game for the County against Essex at Romford in 1957, establishing himself as the number one wicket-keeper the following summer and not missing a game until 1968. Never an exhibitionist, he just got on with the job in a professional and workmanlike manner, collecting 826 victims (707 caught and 119 stumped). On leaving the first-class game he turned to umpiring and has stood in twenty-six Tests, as well as officiating in the 1979 and 1983 World Cup finals.

1958 team. Back row, left to right: H.R. White (masseur), B.D. Wells, A.S. Brown, J.B. Mortimore, D.R. Smith, R.B. Nicholls, B.J. Meyer, E. Aubrey (scorer). Front row: C.A. Milton, T.W. Graveney, G.M. Emmett (captain), C.H.G. Thomas (secretary), C. Cook, D.M. Young. This season was another disappointing one for the County with only five wins and a position of fourteenth in the Championship. In one of the wettest summers on record, only Martin Young who made 1,755 runs didn't struggle, while with the ball, Sam Cook took 100 wickets in the Championship, including 7 for 9 against Derbyshire at Bristol. John Mortimore had his best season so far and came close to performing the double with 844 runs and 97 wickets.

1959 team. Back row, left to right: H.R. White (masseur), D.R. Smith, D.G. Hawkins, A.S. Brown, R.B. Nicholls, J.R. Bernard, B.J. Meyer. Front row: J.B. Mortimore, C.A. Milton, G.M. Emmett, T.W. Graveney (captain), C.H.G. Thomas (secretary), C. Cook, D.M. Young.

The summer of 1959 was a glorious one but with most of Gloucestershire's home wickets taking spin, the County's batsmen didn't have as profitable a time as the opposition batsmen. Only two Gloucestershire batsmen, Martin Young and Arthur Milton, reached 1,000 runs in the Championship. The bowling was a different matter. Though only Tony Brown took 100 wickets in the Championship, Smith, Cook and Mortimore reached the target in all matches. Mortimore did the double for the first time and Tony Brown took 7 for 11 against eventual champions Yorkshire in a remarkable match at Bristol. The match against Essex at Leyton ended in a tie, and though the County had an outside chance of winning the Championship if they collected a maximum 14 points against Worcestershire, they had to be content in finishing as runners-up after collapsing to 26 for 6 in their first innings!

The victorious Gloucestershire team leave the field after beating Yorkshire by an innings and 77 runs at Bristol in August 1959. Without their Test players, the eventual champions Yorkshire were outplayed and their dismissal in the first innings for 35 settled the issue. Gloucestershire recovered from a shaky start to declare at 294 for 8. Yorkshire's amazing collapse on a pitch which had sweated proved so startling that Brown and Smith, bowling unchanged, shot out their rivals in seventy-five minutes with the last six batsmen all registering ducks. Brown achieved the remarkable analysis of 7 wickets for 11 runs in 11 overs. Despite Bolus holding on for almost four hours to score 91, Brown and Smith would not be denied and ensured that Yorkshire were defeated after an hour's play on the third morning.

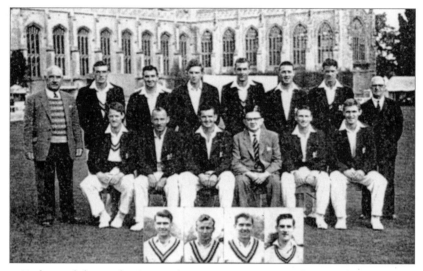

1960 team. Back row, left to right: H.R. White (masseur), D.R. Smith, D.J. A'Court, A.R. Windows, D. Carpenter, B.J. Meyer, R.B. Nicholls, F. Aubrey (scorer). Front row: J.B. Mortimore, C. Cook, T.W. Graveney (captain), C.H.C. Thomas (secretary), D.M. Young, D.G. Hawkins. Inset: A.S. Brown, C.A. Milton, D.A. Allen, C.T.M. Pugh.

After the success of the previous season, it was disappointing that Gloucestershire should slip down to eighth in the Championship. Only Graveney, who missed four games with shoulder trouble, and Young, who hit four centuries, reached four figures in Championship matches.

1961 team. Back row, left to right: H.R. White (masseur), A.S. Brown, D.A. Allen, D.R. Smith, R.B. Nicholls, D. Hobbs, B.J. Meyer, A.R. Windows, F. Dudderidge (scorer). Front row: J.B. Mortimore, C.A. Milton, C.T.M. Pugh (captain), C.H.G. Thomas (secretary), D.M. Young, D.G. Hawkins.

Tom Pugh replaced Tom Graveney as captain and led the County to fifth position in the Championship with eleven wins and eleven defeats in their twenty-eight matches.

The County did well to achieve this position following a series of injuries to key players and Test calls on Milton, Young and Cook. Ron Nicholls moved up to open the batting and responded with 1,602 runs in the Championship. David Allen completed the double with 1,001 runs and 124 wickets, and he bowled well in tandem with John Mortimore. David Smith again took over 100 wickets while Dennis A'Court performed a hat-trick against Derbyshire.

Each year on the anniversary of W.G. Grace's birthday, 18 July, W.S.A. Brown, the Under Sheriff and an old Gloucestershire player, lit a candle of remembrance.

Fred Dudderidge, who retired as Gloucestershire's scorer in 1971, seen here with George Washer of Sussex.

1962 team. Back row, left to right: D.A. Allen, A.S. Brown, A.R. Windows, R.B. Nicholls, R.C. White, D.R. Smith, B.J. Meyer. Front row: F. Dudderidge (scorer), D.M. Young, C. Cook, C.T.M. Pugh (captain), C.A. Milton, J.B. Mortimore, H.R. White (masseur).

This summer saw the County produce identical results to those of 1961, eleven wins and eleven defeats, and with six victories in the last eight matches they finished one position higher in fourth place. Sam Cook headed the national averages with 56 wickets at 17.03 while Tony Brown took 110 wickets in all matches. The batting was much more solid with Arthur Milton hitting four centuries, including 110 not out and 102 not out against Kent at Bristol. Ron Nicholls scored 2,059 runs in all matches and he and Martin Young set a Gloucestershire first wicket record by putting on 395 against Oxford University at The Parks. John Mortimore came close to achieving the double, scoring 1,313 runs and taking 97 wickets, including 8 for 22 against Lancashire.

1963 team. Back row, left to right: R.J.G. McCrudden (secretary), R.B. Nicholls, D.A. Allen, A.S. Brown, A.R. Windows, B.J. Meyer, R.A. White, M. Bissex. Front row: D.M. Young, C.A. Milton, J.K.R. Graveney (captain), C. Cook, J.B. Mortimore.

Having dispensed with the services of Tom Pugh as captain, it was strange to say the least that the County committee should turn to Ken Graveney as his replacement for he was now thirty-eight years old and hadn't played first-class cricket since back trouble forced his retirement in 1951. However, with a number of players well below their form of the previous season, the County dropped to eighth. Arthur Milton again headed the batting and made four Championship hundreds, while John Mortimore achieved the double in all matches. The first of the one-day competitions, the Gillette Cup, was launched this season, but Gloucestershire lost to Middlesex by 39 runs at the first round stage.

Mike Procter (1965–81). Mike Procter and Barry Richards, who was two months older than the Durban-born all-rounder, toured England in 1963 with the South African schoolboys' side. Their performance on this tour, and their consistency in school cricket in South Africa, prompted David Allen to visit both boys' parents and invite them to Gloucestershire for the following summer. They both played local club cricket, second XI cricket and appeared in one first-class match against their own countrymen. At the end of the season both decided to go back to South Africa, but in 1968 when the County were searching for an overseas player it was to Procter that they turned. He had already made his Test debut, taking 15 wickets in three matches against Australia. In his first season with the County, he was in sight of achieving the double of 1,000 runs and 100 wickets when his knee let him down. Procter's development as a cricketer was much influenced by Gloucestershire, because in Procter's time the County needed 100 wickets and 2,000 runs from him.

In 1969 he took 108 wickets, helping Gloucestershire to second place in the Championship, and became one of *Wisden*'s Cricketers of the Year. In 1970 while playing for Rhodesia, Procter hit six consecutive hundreds, the first five in the Currie Cup. His powerful stroke-play brought him many runs, and in 1973 he hit four centuries in the space of eleven days. At the end of that season Gloucestershire won the Gillette Cup, beating Sussex in the final, Procter's contribution being 94 runs and 2 for 27.

In 1977 he hit a century before lunch at Cheltenham and the following year made 203 against Essex, his highest score for the County. Also in 1977 Procter achieved one of the greatest bowling performances ever accomplished in one-day cricket. He performed the hat-trick against Hampshire – Barry Richards, Trevor Jesty and John Rice – as he finished with 6 for 13 to give Gloucestershire victory by 7 runs. Against Leicestershire in 1979 he hit a century before lunch and performed the hat-trick, repeating the bowling feat against Yorkshire in the next match! A marvellous all-rounder, Mike Procter was one of the most entertaining overseas players to have graced the county game.

1964 team. Back row, left to right: F. Dudderidge (scorer), B.J. Meyer, D.W.J. Brown, R.J. Ethridge, A.S. Brown, D.A. Allen, D.R. Smith, H. Jarman. Front row: R.B. Nicholls, J.B. Mortimore, J.K.R. Graveney (captain), C. Cook, D.M. Young.

In what proved to be a dismal season for the County, they finished bottom of the Championship and only won three matches, the first in mid-July. To be fair, they did have bad luck with injuries, the worst being Arthur Milton who broke his arm in the opening match against Oxford University. John Mortimore again completed the double with 1,118 runs and 104 wickets, and along with David Allen appeared in the Test series against Australia.

The last match against Yorkshire at Bristol summed up the County's season. After the visitors had scored 425 for 7 on the first day, rain freshened the wicket and Gloucestershire were dismissed for 47 and 84 on the second day!

1965 team. Back row, left to right: S.E.J. Russell, D.W.J. Brown, M. Bissex, F. Dudderidge (scorer), A.S. Brown, B.J. Meyer, A.R. Windows. Front row: R.B. Nicholls, C.A. Milton, J.B. Mortimore (captain), D.A. Allen, D.R. Smith.

A lot of younger players were introduced this season, so the final position of tenth in the Championship was a welcome change. Mike Bissex with 850 runs and David Brown, who also made nearly 800 runs including his maiden century, were two of the more inexperienced players to shine. David Shepherd made his County debut in the match against Oxford University and hit a quickfire 108. On the bowling front, David Smith took 100 wickets in all matches and Tony Brown 94, while young Bissex's left-arm spin also showed promise.

1966 team. Back row, left to right: S.E.J. Russell, D.W.J. Brown, A.S. Brown, M. Bissex, B.J. Meyer, M.D. Mence, D.G. Bevan. Front row: D.R. Smith, D.A. Allen, R.J.G. McCrudden (secretary), J.B. Mortimore (captain), C.A. Milton, R.B. Nicholls.

The County's misfortunes with injuries continued and helped contribute to a final position of fifteenth. Only two players, Milton and Nicholls, passed 1,000 runs for the season, although Bissex and Brown again showed promise with totals around the 900 mark. When David Smith returned to the County side after missing half the season through injury, he proceeded to show what they had been missing, taking 57 Championship wickets in 13 matches at a cost of 16 runs each. David Allen, who was recalled to the Test side, was the leading wicket-taker with 78 at a cost of under 21 runs each.

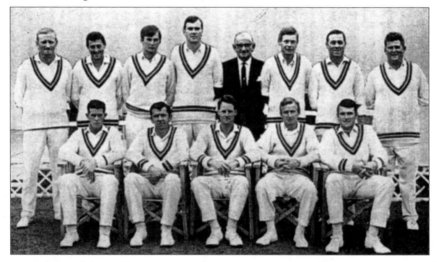

1967 team. Back row, left to right: S.E.J. Russell, D.W.J. Brown, D.G. Bevan, J. Davey, F. Dudderidge (scorer), M. Bissex, B.J. Meyer, D.R. Shepherd. Front row: R.B. Nicholls, D.A. Allen, J.B. Mortimore (captain), C.A. Milton, A.S. Brown.

In yet another disappointing summer for the County, in which they slumped to seventeenth place in the Championship, the batting depended entirely on Milton and Nicholls. Arthur Milton at thirty-nine years of age had the best season of his career, scoring 2,089 runs at an average of 46.62 – more runs than anyone else in the country. Nicholls batted with great consistency, scoring 1,250 runs at a little under 30 and a top score of only 73. The bowlers fared little better, with Mortimore taking 77 wickets and Allen 66, though Jack Davey from Tavistock took 59 wickets at under 27 runs each in his first season.

The 1968 Australian touring team captained by Ian Chappell on a visit to the Whitbread Brewery during their match against Gloucestershire at Bristol. For the record, Ian Redpath scored 135 in Australia's total of 351 for 5 declared, while Arthur Milton hit 155 in Gloucestershire's second innings total of 389 for 6 after they had been bowled out for 172 in the first innings.

The Whitbread Dray Horses enjoying a pint of beer at the Gloucestershire *vs* Australians match at Bristol, July 1968.

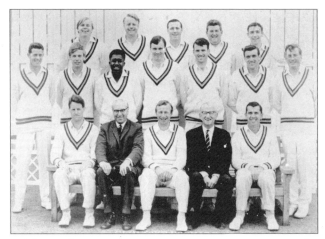

1968 team. Back row, left to right: M.J. Procter, D.M. Green, B.J. Meyer, D.R. Shepherd, H.J. Jarman. Middle row: R.B. Nicholls, M. Bissex, R.W. Phillips, J. Davey, A.S. Brown, D.R. Smith, G.M.M. Wiltshire (coach). Front row: J.B. Mortimore, H.R.S. Bishop (treasurer), C.A. Milton (captain), F. Dudderidge (scorer), D.A. Allen.

Though the season brought only a marginal improvement on 1967 as the County finished sixteenth in the Championship it didn't give a true picture of the cricket played. Rain deprived the County of two certain wins against Surrey and Sussex and thwarted them when they were in strong positions in at least three other fixtures. Former Lancashire player David Green, in his first season with the County, scored 2,137 runs in all matches, 1,875 of them in the Championship. Mike Procter had an outstanding season but because of the wear and tear on his right thigh he didn't bowl again after mid-July. By then he had taken 67 wickets at 16 runs apiece. He did try to bowl against Sussex in the semi-final of the Gillette Cup, which Gloucestershire lost by 48 runs, but then had to return to South Africa for treatment.

1969 team. Back row, left to right: D.M. Green, M.J. Procter, G. Pullar, J. Davey, B.J. Meyer, D.R. Shepherd. Front row: D.R. Smith, J.B. Mortimore, D.A. Allen, C.A. Milton, R.B. Nicholls. (Captain A.S. Brown missing from photograph).

In a season in which there was no theoretical maximum to the number of points a side could score in the Championship, Gloucestershire finished runners-up to Glamorgan in what was a very successful summer. Though the batting was adequate, the bowling was a completely different matter with Mike Procter taking 108 Championship wickets at 15.15 apiece. This summer also saw the introduction of Sunday League cricket, a 40-over competition and sponsored for the first eighteen seasons by John Player. Gloucestershire attained a fairly respectable sixth position, winning eight of their games, although their highest score over the season was 175 for 6 against Northamptonshire.

David Shepherd (1965–79). Between 1959 and 1964 David Shepherd played cricket for Devon, also representing the Minor County side in their match against Australia in 1964. He made his Gloucestershire debut the following year against Oxford University and scored 108. He topped 1,000 runs in a season for the first time in 1968 when he scored 153 against Middlesex, his highest first-class score. Altogether he hit twelve centuries for the County, but perhaps his best innings came in the Gillette Cup second round tie against Surrey at Bristol in 1973. Gloucestershire were 24 for 5, but thanks to Shep's wonderful innings of 72 not out, they finished on 169 for 7 and won by 19 runs.

An important member of the Gloucestershire side throughout the 1970s, many of his better innings were played when the county were in trouble or if they had to bat on an unpredictable wicket. The Gloucestershire faithful loved Shepherd's superstitions, his humour and the most wonderful postures when the score reached 111 – brought to the fore even more nowadays, because of his umpiring and television coverage. He is without doubt one of the leading umpires in world cricket, having officiated in thirty-three Tests and the World Cups of 1987–8, 1991–2 and 1995–6.

diq Mohammed (1972–82). The youngest of a family of five icket-playing brothers, which included both Hanif and ushtaq, he made his debut in Pakistan in the 1959–60 season the age of fourteen, playing for various Karachi sides, kistan International Airways and United Bank. Arriving in ngland in the summer of 1967, he was unable to find a place the Gloucestershire staff as the county were in the process qualifying both Mike Procter and Barry Richards. He later turned for a second trial and made his debut for the first XI 1972, a year after he had played in three Tests for Pakistan on eir tour of England.

Sadiq played in forty-one Tests for Pakistan, hitting his highest st score of 166 against New Zealand at Wellington on the 72–3 tour. A left-handed compact batsman, his favourite ots were the cut and the little dab. He topped the 1,000 run ark on seven occasions with a best of 1,759 runs at an average 47.54 in 1976. He also scored four consecutive centuries in ur consecutive innings, including two centuries in the match ainst Derbyshire. In 1981 he made 203 against Sri Lanka and as awarded a benefit the following summer, his last for the unty.

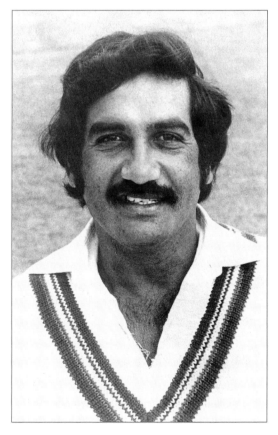

1970 team. Back row, left to right: D.A. Allen, J. Sullivan, M. Bissex, J. Davey, D.M. Green, D.R. Shepherd. Front row: D.R. Smith, J.B. Mortimore, F. Dudderidge (scorer), A.S. Brown (captain), C.A. Milton, R.B. Nicholls, B.J. Meyer.

The County celebrated its centenary this summer but it turned out to be a disastrous season. After finishing as runners-up in the Championship in the previous year, the County plummeted to seventeenth.

Mike Procter was involved in the Rest of the World and England matches and so only played in fifteen out of twenty-four Championship matches. Even then his bowling had lost something of its fire, though he was still the most economical of the Gloucestershire attack. His batting had improved on the previous season and he was well supported by Bissex and Nicholls. David Smith, who took 66 wickets, retired at the end of the season having taken 1,159 wickets in fifteen seasons with the County. Lancashire knocked Gloucestershire out of the Gillette Cup while the County dropped two places to eighth in the Sunday League.

1971 team. Back row, left to right: S.A. Westley, M. Bissex, J. Davey, R.D.V. Knight, J.H. Shackleton, J. Sullivan. Front row: D.M. Green, R.B. Nicholls, M.J. Procter (captain), D.R. Smith, D.R. Shepherd.

Despite an indifferent start to the season, the County proceeded to play such positive cricket that at one time it seemed as if they would win the County Championship, but then rain affected all three Cheltenham Festival games and they had to settle for eighth position.

The star batsman was Mike Procter who scored 1,762 runs at 47.62 ably supported by Nicholls and Knight, who had joined the club from Surrey. Procter was also the leading bowler with Jack Davey and John Mortimore the main supports. Only five wins in the Sunday League meant a drop to sixteenth place, while wins over Sussex and Surrey took Gloucestershire to a Gillette Cup semi-final against Lancashire at Old Trafford. Gloucestershire scored 229 for 6 and Lancashire were 203 for 7 with 6 overs remaining when David Hughes struck 24 runs off one John Mortimore over to win the game for the home side.

Andy Stovold (1973–90). He progressed through Gloucestershire Schools to the England Under-15s and Under-19s sides and with the latter toured India in 1970 as the first-choice wicket-keeper. After touring the West Indies in 1972 with the England Young Cricketers side, he made his debut the following season. During these early years he was keeping wicket and opening the batting. He was to gain instant recognition with the advent of one-day cricket, and in 1977 won the Man-of-the-Match award as Gloucestershire beat Kent in the final of the Benson and Hedges Cup. By 1981 the County had unearthed Jack Russell and so Stovold was able to concentrate on his batting. He responded with 1,338 runs at an average of 34.30 and hit the highest score of his career, 212 not out against Northamptonshire. He started off the 1983 season with 181 against Derbyshire in the opening Championship fixture and ended the summer with 1,671 runs, the highest aggregate of his career.

Now Director of Coaching, his 17,460 runs at an average of 30.00 and 312 victims (268 caught and 44 stumped) are testimony to the claim that he was unlucky not to play for England at least in the one-day game.

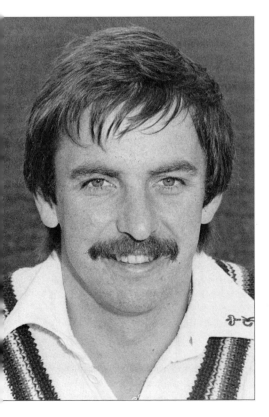

David Graveney (1972–90). The son of Ken Graveney who played for Gloucestershire from 1947 to 1964, David took over the County captaincy from Mike Procter in July 1981 and was appointed captain for 1982, a position he kept until the disappointments towards the end of the 1988 season. Never one to shirk a challenge, Graveney would keep his spirits up even when things were going wrong. His tactical skill was extremely sound, though there were some who said he didn't bowl himself enough, but it was difficult for him when John Childs was in the side. His left-arm spin was never quite good enough to win an England cap but his 815 wickets at 29.06 apiece are testimony to his worth to Gloucestershire. His best figures were 8 for 85 against Nottinghamshire at Cheltenham in 1974 and his best match figures 14 for 165 against Worcestershire at Bristol in 1988, after which he was dismissed as captain!

After playing his last game for the County in 1990, he joined Somerset for a season before he committed himself to the most arduous task in the game – the captaincy of Durham. Now Chairman of the England selectors, David Graveney has served the game with great dignity over the last twenty-six years.

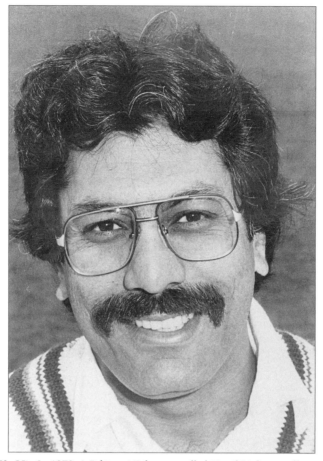

Zaheer Abbas (1972–85). In 1970–1 Pakistani Zaheer equalled Hanif Mohammed's record by scoring five centuries in six matches, his highest score being 202 against Intikhab's Karachi side. Those five hundreds went a long way towards helping Zaheer reach his first goal, the 1971 touring party to England. In the opening fixture of that tour, he hit 110 off the Worcestershire attack. Then in the first Test (only the second of his career) he achieved his wildest dream, scoring 274. He was a target for many of the counties, but to Gloucestershire's delight he opted for them. In his early days with the County, he wore gold-rimmed spectacles, later switching to contact lenses. Even then he had most of the shots, playing them with great ease and immense power. In 1975 he was awarded his county cap; both he and the Gloucestershire faithful thought it would have arrived earlier. After all, Zaheer was a world-class player. He liked nothing better than breaking batting records and quite openly admitted it: 'I have always wanted to be respected in the cricket world and by its historians in later years.'

His fondness for playing long innings often put a great strain on his lean physique. During an English season he would consume porridge and Guinness to build up his stamina, completely oblivious to the comments of his Gloucestershire team-mates.

In 1976, against Surrey at the Oval, he scored 216 not out and 156 not out. His match aggregate of 372 runs is the highest in England by a batsman without being dismissed. He performed this feat of hitting a double century and a century on four occasions. Throughout this summer Zaheer headed the national averages, scoring 2,554 runs at 75.11 including eleven centuries, one of which at Worcester was scored before lunch. In 1982 he became only the twentieth player in the history of the game to score a hundred centuries, doing so at Lahore in the first Test against India. Zaheer played in seventy-eight Tests, scoring 5,062 runs at 44.79.

A prince among batsmen, he finally called it a day in 1985, and was sorely missed by cricket lovers in general and Gloucestershire supporters in particular.

1972 team. Back row, left to right: Zaheer Abbas, D.R. Shepherd, D.A. Allen, J.H. Shackleton, R.D.V. Knight, A.G. Avery (scorer), J. Davey, B.J. Meyer, G.G.M. Wiltshire (coach), M. Bissex. Front row: J.C. Foat, Sadiq Mohammed, J.B. Mortimore, A.S. Brown (captain), G.W. Parker (secretary), M.J. Procter, C.A. Milton, R.B. Nicholls, R. Swetman.

Pakistan Test players Zaheer Abbas and Sadiq Mohammed strengthened the County side for this summer and though neither did anything particularly outstanding in their first season with the club, they did over the next decade or so. This season the County finished third in the Championship thanks mainly to bowling performances of a high quality. The County finished sixteenth in the Sunday League and lost to Kent in the first round of the Gillette Cup. This was also the first season of the Benson and Hedges Cup in which Gloucestershire reached the semi-finals before losing to Yorkshire. One of the best performances in the competition came from Procter, who scored an unbeaten 154 out of a total of 215 against Somerset in just 130 minutes!

1973 team. Back row, left to right: G.G.M. Wiltshire (coach), D.R. Shepherd, J.C. Foat, R.D.V. Knight, D.A. Graveney, J. Davey, Zaheer Abbas, M.S.T. Dunstan, A.G. Avery (scorer). Front row: Sadiq Mohammed, M.J. Procter, F.J. Twizleton (chairman), A.S. Brown (captain), G.W. Parker (secretary), J.B. Mortimore, A.W. Stovold.

This summer Gloucestershire had an excellent all-round season. The County finished fifth in the Championship with Mike Procter scoring 1,351 runs at an average of 64.33 and six centuries. Sadiq Mohammed also had a good season, scoring over 1,200 runs, hitting three Championship centuries and a magnificent 184 against New Zealand at Bristol. The County might have done even better if Procter's injury hadn't limited him to bowling just 238 overs, taking only 26 wickets. Though the County failed to qualify for the Benson and Hedges quarter-finals, they climbed to sixth in the Sunday League. The high spot of the season was the Gillette Cup. After beating Glamorgan, Surrey, Essex and Worcestershire, the County met Sussex in the final at Lord's. Victory by 40 runs gave Gloucestershire their first major trophy since 1877.

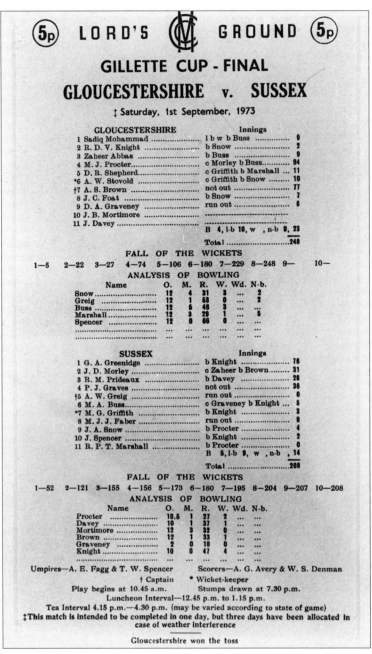

GILLETTE CUP - FINAL
GLOUCESTERSHIRE v. SUSSEX
‡ Saturday, 1st September, 1973

GLOUCESTERSHIRE — Innings

		Runs
1 Sadiq Mohammad	l b w b Buss	9
2 R. D. V. Knight	b Snow	2
3 Zaheer Abbas	b Buss	9
4 M. J. Procter	c Morley b Buss	94
5 D. R. Shepherd	c Griffith b Marshall	11
*6 A. W. Stovold	c Griffith b Snow	10
†7 A. S. Brown	not out	77
8 J. C. Foat	b Snow	7
9 D. A. Graveney	run out	6
10 J. B. Mortimore		
11 J. Davey		
	B 4, l-b 10, w , n-b 9,	23
	Total	248

FALL OF THE WICKETS
1—5   2—22   3—27   4—74   5—106   6—180   7—229   8—248   9—   10—

ANALYSIS OF BOWLING

Name	O.	M.	R.	W.	Wd.	N-b.
Snow	12	4	31	3	...	2
Greig	12	1	53	0	...	2
Buss	12	5	46	3	...	..
Marshall	12	3	29	1	...	5
Spencer	12	0	66	0	...	...

SUSSEX — Innings

		Runs
1 G. A. Greenidge	b Knight	76
2 J. D. Morley	c Zaheer b Brown	31
3 R. M. Prideaux	b Davey	28
4 P. J. Graves	not out	36
†5 A. W. Greig	run out	0
6 M. A. Buss	c Graveney b Knight	5
*7 M. G. Griffith	b Knight	3
8 M. J. J. Faber	run out	9
9 J. A. Snow	b Procter	4
10 J. Spencer	b Knight	2
11 R. P. T. Marshall	b Procter	0
	B 5, l-b 9, w , n-b ,	14
	Total	208

FALL OF THE WICKETS
1—52   2—121   3—155   4—156   5—173   6—180   7—195   8—204   9—207   10—208

ANALYSIS OF BOWLING

Name	O.	M.	R.	W.	Wd.	N-b.
Procter	10.5	1	27	2	...	...
Davey	10	1	37	1	...	...
Mortimore	12	3	32	0	...	...
Brown	12	1	33	1	...	...
Graveney	2	0	18	0	...	...
Knight	10	0	47	4	...	...

Umpires—A. E. Fagg & T. W. Spencer   Scorers—A. G. Avery & W. S. Denman

† Captain   * Wicket-keeper

Play begins at 10.45 a.m.   Stumps drawn at 7.30 p.m.

Luncheon Interval—12.45 p.m. to 1.15 p.m.

Tea Interval 4.15 p.m.—4.30 p.m. (may be varied according to state of game)

‡This match is intended to be completed in one day, but three days have been allocated in case of weather interference

Gloucestershire won the toss

Gillette Cup Final Scorecard, 1973. Having won the toss and elected to bat, Gloucestershire lost Sadiq, Knight and Zaheer to the pace of John Snow and Michael Buss and were 27 for 3. Procter then came to the rescue, driving and hooking at every opportunity, but after two-and-a-half hours at the crease he was caught by Morley at deep square leg for 94. Then captain Tony Brown played a decisive innings of 77 not out, hitting 46 out of the last 68 runs added in the last 8 overs as Gloucestershire totalled 248 for 8 in their 60 overs.

Sussex openers Greenidge and Morley were not overawed by Gloucestershire's total and added 52 for the first wicket. Gloucestershire's opponents reached 155 for 2 and seemed to be in with a good chance of victory, but after Jack Davey bowled Prideaux and Jim Foat superbly ran out Tony Greig, the innings fell away – and in the end Gloucestershire won comfortably by 40 runs.

Geoffrey Greenidge, the Sussex opener who top scored in his side's Gillette Cup Final total of 208 with an innings of 76, is bowled by Gloucestershire's Roger Knight. The umpire walking in from square leg is former Kent player Arthur Fagg.

The Banner Boys: a selection of Gloucestershire supporters at Chelmsford for the Gillette Cup quarter-final against Essex in 1973. The match proved a comfortable win for Gloucestershire who, after totalling 236 for 9, won by 30 runs.

The Gillette Cup Winners' pennant presented to the County after their 40-run win over Sussex in 1973.

Mr Alf Rich, the Lord Mayor of Gloucester, seen kissing the Gillette Cup just before the team's open-top bus ride through the city.

Pictured on Gloucester's Eastgate Street are the 1973 Gillette Cup winners, touring the county in an open-top bus. Captain and Man-of-the-Match Tony Brown has the trophy firmly in his grasp, while other players facing the camera include John Mortimore, Jack Davey, David Graveney, Mike Procter, David Shepherd and Roger Knight.

The victorious Gloucestershire side visiting the BAC Concorde mock-up at Filton, after winning the Gillette Cup in 1973.

When the West Indies played Gloucestershire at Cheltenham in 1973, they found themselves short of a scorer. Local lady Jill Howells stepped into the breach and obviously did a good job, her work meeting with approval from Alvin Kallicharran, Ron Headley, Elquemedo Willett and captain Rohan Kanhai. For the record, the match was drawn, Gloucestershire scoring 213 for 9 declared and 93 for 7 declared, and the West Indies replying with 104 for 6, 6 runs short with 4 wickets left!

Brian Brain (1976–81). Brian Brain was a fine professional, always ready to bowl and a glutton for work. He made his first-class debut for Worcestershire in 1959 but left the staff the following year. He rejoined in 1963 and reappeared in the first XI the following summer. He was awarded his county cap in 1966 but five years later left the staff for a second time, only to return in 1973. It was then that he began to produce his best form for the County, taking 84 Championship wickets in that summer of 1973. But in 1975 after he had taken 508 wickets at 24.20 each, he was dismissed. It was a great shock to the Worcestershire members, for he had had three very successful seasons after returning from injury.

Brain was thirty-six years old when he joined Gloucestershire for the 1976 season, and though he was virtually in the twilight of his career he proceeded over the next six seasons to take 316 wickets at 24.98, with a best of 7 for 51 against the Australians at Bristol in 1977. It was a fine achievement, for this most popular of players was hampered by injuries in his last year with the County, limiting his victims to sixteen.

1974 team. Back row, left to right: A.G. Avery (scorer), Zaheer Abbas, M.S.T. Dunstan, J.H. Shackleton, R.D.V. Knight, D.A. Graveney, J. Davey, D.R. Shepherd, Sadiq Mohammed. Front row: R.B. Nicholls, M.J. Procter, A.S. Brown (captain), J.B.Mortimore, R. Swetman.

With Zaheer and Sadiq touring England with Pakistan and so only available to play in four matches, the County slipped to fourteenth in the Championship. Roger Knight was the only batsman to exceed 1,000 runs, hitting four Championship centuries in the process. Though Procter finished fifth in the national bowling averages, he only took 39 wickets. In the one-day competitions, performances were even gloomier. The County failed to qualify for the knockout stages of the Benson and Hedges Cup, finished twelfth in the Sunday League and lost to Lancashire at Bristol in their first match in the Gillette Cup.

1975 team. Back row: D.A. Graveney, J.H. Dixon, R.D.V. Knight, J.Davey. Middle row: A.G. Avery (scorer), G.G.M. Wiltshire (coach), Sadiq Mohammed, J.C. Foat, A.J. Brassington, J.H. Childs, Zaheer Abbas, A.W. Stovold, N.H. Finan, J.H. Shackleton. Front row: D.R. Shepherd, G.W. Parker (secretary), A.S. Brown (captain), M.J. Procter.

This was another disappointing season for the County with injuries again dominating the scene. As in the previous season, Gloucestershire only won four matches but ended the season in sixteenth place in the Championship. Zaheer and Sadiq returned to the side, and both had good seasons scoring 1,426 and 1,268 runs respectively, but Procter was only able to play in four games following his winter knee operation.

The County again failed to qualify for the knockout stages of the Benson and Hedges Cup, winning only one of its qualifying matches, and slipped to fifteenth in the Sunday League. In the Gillette Cup Gloucestershire beat Oxfordshire and Leicestershire, where both Zaheer and Sadiq made centuries before losing to Lancashire at Old Trafford by 3 wickets, with the home side having just three balls to spare.

1976 team. Back row, left to right: N.H.C. Cooper, J.C. Foat, A.J. Brassington, J.H. Childs, J. Davey, J.H. Shackleton, D.A. Graveney, J.H. Dixon, B.M. Brain, N.H. Finan, G.G.M. Wiltshire (coach), A.W. Stovold, A.G. Avery (scorer). Front row: Zaheer Abbas, D.R. Shepherd, A.S. Brown (captain), J.K.R. Graveney (chairman), M.J. Procter, Sadiq Mohammed.

The main feature of this season in which Gloucestershire finished third in the Championship was the outstanding form of Zaheer Abbas. He topped the national averages with 2,431 runs at 78.41 and hit eleven centuries, including a top score of 230 not out against Kent at Canterbury. Mike Procter scored 1,005 runs and took 63 wickets to be one of the country's leading all-rounders. In the one-day competitions Gloucestershire again disappointed. They finished bottom of the Sunday League, failed to reach the knockout stages of the Benson and Hedges Cup, and though they beat Worcestershire and Yorkshire in the early rounds of the Gillette Cup, they were easily beaten at Old Trafford in the quarter-final.

1977 team. Back row, left to right: A.J. Hignell, J.C. Foat, B.M. Brain, J.H. Shackleton, M.J. Vernon, J.H. Childs. Front row: D.A. Graveney, Sadiq Mohammed, M.J. Procter (captain), D.R. Shepherd, Zaheer Abbas, A.W. Stovold.

In what was the first year of Mike Procter's captaincy, Gloucestershire again finished third in the Championship, just five points adrift of Middlesex and Kent who shared the title. The side can consider themselves unlucky as their matches against Northamptonshire at Gloucester and Yorkshire at Bristol were abandoned without a ball being bowled.

Zaheer topped the batting averages with 1,579 runs at 56.39, and in the match against Sussex at Cheltenham scored 205 not out and 108 not out. Mike Procter had a brilliant season with the ball taking 108 wickets in the Championship at 17.83 each.

Though they went out of the Gillette Cup at an early stage, they finished sixth in the Sunday League. After qualifying for the quarter-finals of the Benson and Hedges Cup, the County beat Middlesex before disposing of Hampshire at Southampton in the semi-final by 8 runs. In the final at Lord's, Kent were beaten by 64 runs to give Gloucestershire their first success in the competition.

The 1977 Benson and Hedges Cup winners' pennant awarded to the County after they had beaten Kent by 64 runs in the Final. Below the pennant is the scorecard for the match.

Mike Procter is chaired by David Shepherd and David Graveney. Zaheer Abbas is in the foreground and, behind him, Julian Shackleton; on Graveney's left are Sadiq Mohammed, Brian Brain, David Partridge and Ian Crawford. Gloucestershire won the toss and soon assumed control with Andy Stovold and Zaheer Abbas the major run-getters in a total of 237 for 6. A superb spell of opening bowling by Procter and Brain dented Kent's hopes of scoring just over 4 runs per over needed for victory. Despite fine efforts by Woolmer and Shepherd, Kent were bowled out for 173, leaving Gloucestershire the winners by 64 runs. Towards the end of the game, play was held up several times as Gloucestershire fans invaded the pitch in excitement, and when the trophy was presented to Mike Procter in front of the pavilion the fans had to be forced back by squads of police.

Phil Bainbridge (1977–90). Though he made his Gloucestershire debut in 1977, it wasn't until 1981 that he played his first full season. He scored 1,019 runs and took 33 wickets, and was nominated as the Commercial Union's Under-23 Batsman of the Year. In 1984–5 he was selected to tour Zimbabwe with the England Counties side. At the end of the following summer, in which he scored 1,456 runs at 58.24 to top the County's batting averages, he was chosen as one of *Wisden's* five Cricketers of the Year. In 1986 he had a memorable weekend as Gloucestershire entertained Somerset at Bristol. In the County Championship his right-arm medium-pacers brought him his best figures of 8 for 53, while in the Sunday League he hit an unbeaten 106. In 1988 he hit the highest score of his career, 169 against Yorkshire at Cheltenham, and in 1989 he was awarded a benefit.

A consistent, dependable performer, he scored 12,281 runs at 34.11, and took 273 wickets at 36.46 before leaving to play for Durham.

Chris Broad (1979–94). Bristol-born Chris Broad was tried as an opener in the absence of Pakistani Test player Sadiq Mohammed, but in the early stages of his career he preferred batting a little lower down the order. In 1980 he hit a century before lunch in the match against Oxford University and in 1983 hit the highest score of his Gloucestershire career, 145 against Nottinghamshire at Bristol. At the end of that summer Broad left the County to play for Nottinghamshire, believing there was a more ambitious approach at Trent Bridge and that his Test prospects would improve.

With Nottinghamshire he appeared in four finals at Lord's but the highlight of his career was England's successful Australian tour of 1986–7 under Mike Gatting. He scored hundreds in successive Tests at Perth, Adelaide and Melbourne and won the International Cricketer of the Year award. He returned to the West Country in 1993 after Nottinghamshire had dismissed him. Not everyone at Bristol approved, but after two seasons in which he took his career total of runs for Gloucestershire to 6,549 at 31.79, an arthritic hip condition forced his retirement.

1978 team. Back row, left to right: A.G. Avery (scorer), B.M. Brain, J.H. Shackleton, N.H. Finan, A.J. Brassington, J.C. Foat, N.H.C. Cooper, I.C. Crawford, S.J. Windaybank, J.H. Childs, G.G.M. Wiltshire (coach). Front row: A.W. Stovold, J. Davey, M.J. Procter (captain), A.S. Brown (secretary), D.R. Shepherd, D.A. Graveney.

Following the success of the previous summer, hopes were high. However, the County had one of its most disappointing seasons. Procter, who scored 1,625 runs including 203 against Essex at Gloucester and took 69 wickets, had another marvellous season. He was well supported by Zaheer Abbas who hit 213 against Sussex at Hove. Brian Brain also bowled well, taking 64 wickets, but despite all their efforts the County dropped to tenth. They finished bottom of the John Player League, failed to qualify from their group in the Benson and Hedges Cup and went out in the first round of the Gillette Cup, as Lancashire's Clive and David Lloyd hit centuries in an 8 wicket win for the red-rose county.

1979 team. Back row, left to right: M.A. Garnham, A.J. Hignell, J.C. Foat, G.G.M. Wiltshire (coach), P. Bainbridge, A.J. Brassington, N.H. Finan, M.D. Partridge, B.M. Brain, J.H. Childs, A.G. Avery (scorer), B.C. Broad, S.J. Windaybank, M.W. Stovold. Front row: A.W. Stovold, Zaheer Abbas, A.S. Brown (secretary), M.J. Procter (captain), D.R. Shepherd, Sadiq Mohammed, D.A. Graveney.

Gloucestershire again ended the season in tenth place in the Championship with Mike Procter in fine form, scoring 1,200 runs at 38.70 and capturing 74 wickets at 20.14 runs apiece. Sadiq Mohammed with 1,504 runs at 60.16 was the pick of the batsmen, though it was the South African all-rounder whose talents helped the County win five games in the Championship. Once again no progress was made in either the Benson and Hedges or Gillette Cup competitions, but the County moved up to eighth in the Sunday League after winning seven of its matches.

1980 team. Back row, left to right: A.G. Avery (scorer), I. Broome, D. Surridge, J.H. Childs, A.J. Wright, B.C. Broad, M.D. Partridge, S.J. Windaybank, P. Bainbridge, A.J. Wilkins, M.W. Stovold. Front row: A.J. Brassington, A.W. Stovold, Zaheer Abbas, B.M. Brain, M.J. Procter (captain), Sadiq Mohammed, D.A. Graveney, G.G.M. Wiltshire (coach).

In another wet summer, Gloucestershire moved up to seventh in the Championship despite winning one game fewer than the previous season. Zaheer Abbas headed the County's batting with 1,296 runs at 38.11, while Mike Procter, who was not always fit to bowl, took 48 wickets at 17.85 runs each. The County made an early exit from the Gillette Cup, losing by 8 runs against Surrey at The Oval and once again failed to qualify for the knockout stages of the Benson and Hedges Cup. In the Sunday League the County again won seven matches, but ended the season in tenth place.

1981 team. Back row, left to right: A.S. Brown (secretary/manager), P. Bainbridge, J.H. Childs, B.C. Broad, D. Surridge, S.J. Windaybank, A.W. Stovold, A.G. Avery (scorer). Front row: M.W. Stovold, Zaheer Abbas, D.A. Graveney, A.J. Hignell, Sadiq Mohammed, A.J. Wilkins.

Though the County had a disappointing season, dropping from seventh to thirteenth in the Championship, finishing sixteenth in the Sunday League and having little success in the Benson and Hedges and newly named Nat West Cup competitions, it was a marvellous season for Zaheer Abbas. The Pakistani Test player topped the national batting averages, scoring 2,230 runs at 85.76 and with a top score of 215 not out against Somerset at Bath. He hit 1,000 runs in the month of June, thus becoming the third Gloucestershire player after Grace and Hammond to achieve that feat.

Jack Russell (1981–). His cricket developed both at Stroud CC and at Archway Comprehensive, where he captained, opened the batting and bowled but never tried his hand at wicket-keeping! He played his first county match when he was seventeen against Sri Lanka at Bristol, taking seven catches and making a stumping. In 1983, his first full season, he made a great impression, scoring 507 runs and dismissing sixty-three batsmen (forty-six caught and seventeen stumped) as he emerged as a genuine all-rounder. Awarded his county cap in 1985, he hit his first century for Gloucestershire the following summer when he made 108 against Worcestershire at Hereford in the Sunday League. In 1987 he scored 779 runs at 28.85 and dismissed fifty-eight batsmen in County Championship matches.

He was chosen to tour Pakistan in 1987–8 with the England team, but only played in one match and that wasn't a Test. However, as understudy to Bruce French, he had plenty of time on his hands to pursue his hobby of line drawing. Before he had departed a local art dealer in Bristol had noted his creativity on the canvas and had offered to set up an exhibition of Russell's material when he returned. He was swamped by demands for limited editions and commissions for cricketing scenes and portraits. He eventually made his Test debut against Sri Lanka in 1988 in what was also David Lawrence's first match, and after going in as night-watchman made 94, the highest individual score of the match.

He came of age against the Australians in the Test series of 1989, emerging as England's Man of the Series. At Old Trafford he hit his maiden Test hundred, an unbeaten 128, and at the end of the summer was chosen as one of Wisden's five Cricketers of the Year. Jack has at the time of writing played in forty-nine Tests for England. Captain of Gloucestershire in 1995, he has up to the end of the 1997 season scored 10,137 runs for the County and helped dismiss 761 batsmen (674 caught and 87 stumped).

1982 team. Back row, left to right: P. Bainbridge, P.W. Romaines, A.J. Wright, B.C. Broad, F.D. Stephenson, D. Surridge, J.N. Shepherd, R.C. Russell, A.G. Avery (scorer). Front row: B. Dudleston, D.A. Graveney (captain), A.S. Brown (secretary/manager), J.H. Childs, A.W. Stovold.

This summer saw the County drop two places to fifteenth in the Championship despite Zaheer Abbas scoring 667 runs in 11 completed innings at an average of 60.63. He was well supported by Bainbridge, Sadiq and Stovold, who hit a career best 212 not out against Northamptonshire. John Shepherd was the pick of the bowlers, taking 63 wickets, but age was against the thirty-eight-year-old West Indian Test player.

The County finished fourteenth in the Sunday League, and though they won two group matches in the Benson and Hedges Cup they failed to qualify for the knockout stages. In the Nat West Trophy they beat Nottinghamshire by 9 wickets, but lost to Middlesex in the quarter-final by 3 runs, when a four off the last ball would have given them victory!

1983 team. Back row, left to right: R.C. Russell, P. Bainbridge, E.J. Cunningham, A.J. Wright, R.J. Doughty, B. Dudleston, K.E. Rice. Middle row: D.G. Collier (secretary), G.G.M. Wiltshire (coach), D.V. Lawrence, B.C. Broad, G.E. Sainsbury, D.P. Simpkins, F.R. Tracey, A.J. Brassington, P.W. Romaines, A.G. Avery (scorer). Front row: A.J. Hignell, J.N. Shepherd, D.A.Graveney (captain), Zaheer Abbas, A.W. Stovold, J.H. Childs.

The County made a slight improvement in the Championship moving up three places to twelfth. Six batsmen passed the 1,000 run mark with Andy Stovold leading the way with 1,592 runs including four centuries. John Shepherd again had a good all-round season, scoring 1,025 runs at 36.60 and taking 67 wickets at 30.55 runs each. In the Sunday League Gloucestershire again finished in fourteenth place, while they reached the quarter-finals of both the Benson and Hedges Cup and Nat West Trophy competitions.

Don Perry, a former notable club cricketer from Cheltenham, was Gloucestershire County Cricket Club Chairman from 1982–9 and President from 1992–5.

Gloucestershire and Middlesex teams being entertained by the Lord Mayor of Bristol at the Mansion House, 1983. Only four overs of the Benson and Hedges Cup quarter-final match were bowled and Middlesex went through on the toss of a coin. The TCCB were unsympathetic to pleas of captains David Graveney and Mike Gatting who wanted the game decided by some sort of a cricket match later in the season.

1984 team. Back row, left to right: R.C. Russell, C.W.J. Athey, A.J. Wright, P.W. Romaines, J.W. Lloyds, R. Payne. Middle row: G.G.M. Wiltshire (coach), P.H. Twizzell, D.V. Lawrence, E.J. Cunningham, G.E. Sainsbury, D.A. Burrows, K.M. Curran, A.G. Avery (scorer). Front row: A.J. Brassington, J.N. Shepherd, D.A. Graveney (captain), D.G. Collier (secretary), P. Bainbridge, A.W. Stovold.

This season was a disastrous one for the County as they won only one game in the Championship and finished in bottom place. Yet despite this Bill Athey, in his first season with the County following his arrival from Yorkshire, and Durham-born Paul Romaines both passed 1,800 runs for the season. The County finished thirteenth in the Sunday League and won only one of its Benson and Hedges qualifying matches. In the Nat West Trophy Staffordshire were beaten by 8 wickets, but then Lancashire won easily in the next round.

1985 team. Back row, left to right: J.W. Lloyds, B.F. Davison, A.J. Wright, C.A. Walsh, D.V. Lawrence, K.M. Curran, R.G.P .Ellis, R.C. Russell. Front row: P.W. Romaines, P. Bainbridge, D.A. Graveney (captain), A.J. Brassington, C.W.J. Athey.

With the full-time availability of Courtney Walsh and David Lawrence, there was a remarkable upturn in the County's fortunes as they finished third in the Championship. Walsh took 82 wickets and Lawrence 79 while Gary Sainsbury's 21 wickets at 18.09 runs each put him third in the national averages. Phil Bainbridge had a good season with the bat, scoring 1,456 runs at 58.24. The County finished in joint sixth place in the Sunday League, and though they failed to qualify for the later stages of the Benson and Hedges Cup they reached the quarter-final of the Nat West Trophy, where they lost to Northamptonshire in a high scoring match.

vid Lawrence (1981–). Gloucester-born David Lawrence
s a consistently hostile bowler, though his strength, pace and
olehearted approach didn't always bring him the figures he
served. A perfect foil for Courtney Walsh, his best season
s 1985 when he took 79 wickets in the Championship at
.34 runs apiece. In 1988 he produced the best figures of his
eer, 7 for 47 against Surrey at Cheltenham – just one of a
mber of outstanding bowling performances that led to him
nning his first Test cap against Sri Lanka towards the end of
t season.

he first English-born black cricketer to represent his county
his country, he terrorised the Sri Lankan batsmen and was
sperately unlucky to collect only 3 wickets in the match.
bbed 'Syd' after the late band leader, he sustained a freak
ury, after skidding in the footholes at the popping crease on
gland's 1992 tour of New Zealand. The result: one badly
attered kneecap. Many feared they'd never again see the
stling bowling style which made him a great favourite on the
unty circuit, but they hadn't reckoned on his iron will, for in
97, after an absence of five seasons, he returned to county
cket.

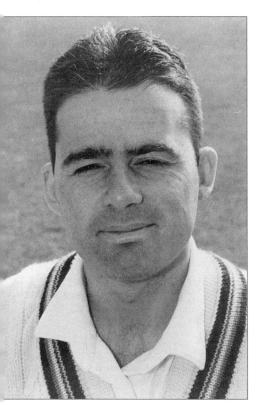

Tony Wright (1982–). The Stevenage-born right-handed
batsman had come to Gloucestershire as a sixteen-year-old in
1978 but had to wait a further four years before making his
first team debut. It was 1984 before he began to produce the
goods, scoring 971 runs at 26.97 and hitting his maiden first-
class century, 139 against Surrey at Cheltenham.

Improving season by season, he was awarded his county cap
in 1987, the season he passed the 1,000 run mark for the first
of what is now six occasions. He was appointed County captain
in 1990, a position he held for four seasons. In 1991 he topped
the County averages with 1,596 runs at 45.60, including three
centuries. He repeated the feat in 1994 and in 1995 scored
1,401 runs at 46.70. That season he scored four hundreds
including the highest score of his career, 193 against
Nottinghamshire at Bristol. Recently plagued by injuries, he
has at the time of writing scored 13,095 runs for
Gloucestershire at an average of 29.36.

1986 team. Back row, left to right: K.P. Tomlins, A.J. Wright, P.W. Romaines, D.V. Lawrence, G.E. Sainsbury, K.M. Curran, V.S. Greene, J.W. Lloyds, A.J. Brassington. Front row: M.W. Alleyne, C.A. Walsh, J.N. Shepherd, D.A. Graveney (captain), P. Bainbridge, A.W. Stovold, C.W.J. Athey, R.C. Russell.

Despite a dismal showing in the one-day game where the County finished bottom of the Sunday League, failed to make the knockout stages of the Benson and Hedges Cup and were knocked out in the second round of the Nat West Trophy, they finished runners-up to Essex in the Championship. The County only lost three matches and two of these came in the final few weeks of the season as they chased virtually impossible targets in matches where the weather had intervened. The find of the season was Mark Alleyne, who at the age of eighteen, scored 116 not out against Sussex to become the youngest player in the County's history to make a century. Courtney Walsh also had a magnificent summer, taking 118 Championship wickets at 18.17 each, with a best performance of 9 for 72 against Somerset at Bristol.

1987 team. Back row, left to right: R.C. Russell, J.W. Lloyds, M.W. Alleyne, O.C.K. Smith, D.W. Taylor, A.J. Wright, K.P. Tomlins. Middle row: A.G. Avery (scorer), C.W.J. Athey, A.J. Brassington, G.E. Sainsbury, D.V. Lawrence, D.A. Burrows, P.W. Romaines, L. Bardsley (physiotherapist). Front row: A.W. Stovold, P.G.M. August (secretary), D.A. Graveney (captain), D.N. Perry (chairman), P. Bainbridge, J.N. Shepherd.

A series of injuries to key players hampered the County's progress this season and so they had to be content with finishing tenth in the Championship. Courtney Walsh looked tired after three years continuous cricket and though he missed three matches while playing for the Rest of the World XI, his tally of wickets dropped to 59. Bill Athey was the pick of the batsmen, hitting five centuries – four in succession and a 98 in the last six weeks of the summer. There was, however, an upturn in the County's one-day performances, as they finished third in the Sunday League, lost off the last ball to Kent in the quarter-finals of the Benson and Hedges Cup and reached the semi-finals of the Nat West Trophy.

ll Athey (1984–92). Middlesbrough-born Bill Athey began
s first-class career with Yorkshire in 1976 but after eight
asons in which he scored 6,320 runs at an average of 28.08 he
ft the strife-torn county to join Gloucestershire. He had an
cellent first season in 1984 scoring 1,812 runs at 37.75 and
er the next nine seasons proved himself to be a prolific scorer
county cricket with 11,383 runs at an average of 42.63.
hough he played in twenty-three Tests for England, he all too
equently failed at the highest level. In 1986–7 he was
romoted to open the innings in Australia and enjoyed his one
ccessful series. The following summer he scored 123 against
kistan in the Lord's Test but managed only one other 50 in 31
nings.

Ironically in 1992 he made his highest score for the County,
1 against Sussex at Cheltenham, the county he joined the
llowing season.

Diana, Princess of Wales, a Gloucestershire County Cricket Club patron, sat alongside Grahame Parker
OBE (Gloucestershire CCC President 1986–7) at a club function at the Cheltenham Town Hall in 1987.

1988 team. Back row, left to right: I.P. Butcher, J.W. Lloyds, A.J. Wright, N.W. Pooley, V.S. Greene, M.W. Alleyne, P.W. Romaines. Middle row: J.N. Shepherd (coach), D.J. Thomas, A.J. Brassington, D.V. Lawrence, D.J. Chubb, K.B.S. Jarvis, T.M. Alderman, K.M.Curran, G.G.M. Wiltshire (coach). Front row: K.B. Ibadulla, A.W. Stovold, P.G.M. August (secretary), D.A. Graveney (captain), D.N. Perry (chairman), P. Bainbridge, C.W.J. Athey, R.C. Russell.

The County retained tenth position in the Championship with Terry Alderman replacing Courtney Walsh, who was touring with the West Indies. The Australian Test star took 75 wickets but the bowling averages were headed by Kevin Curran who took 65 wickets at 21.30 each. The Zimbabwean all-rounder also scored 1,005 runs at 37.22 to complete an outstanding season. Bill Athey was again the County's leading batsman, scoring 1,037 runs at 74.07, although both Stovold and Bainbridge exceeded his total of runs. Though the County failed to qualify for the knockout stages of the Benson and Hedges Cup and were knocked out in the quarter-finals of the Nat West Trophy, they did finish the season as runners-up to Worcestershire in the Sunday League.

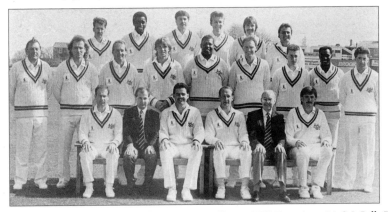

1989 team. Back row, left to right: G.A. Tedstone, M.W. Alleyne, P.W. Romaines, M.C.J. Ball, R.C. Russell, K.B. Ibadulla. Middle row: G.G.M. Wiltshire (coach), I.P. Butcher, J.W. Lloyds, K.M. Curran, D.V. Lawrence, K.B.S. Jarvis, M.W. Pooley, V.S. Greene, P. Bainbridge. Front row: A.W. Stovold, P.G.M. August (secretary), A.J. Wright, (captain), C.W.J. Athey, D.N. Perry (chairman), D.A. Graveney.

Though the County moved up one place in the Championship to ninth, eleven matches were lost and many of them in disastrous circumstances. The worst was probably the game against Hampshire at Portsmouth where Gloucestershire were bowled out for 48 on a good batting wicket after the home side had declared at 406 for 9! The County finished sixteenth in the Sunday League and went out to Worcestershire in the first round of the Nat West Trophy. In the Benson and Hedges Cup the County topped its group, winning all four matches before losing to Nottinghamshire by 5 runs in the quarter-final, with former County player Chris Broad hitting a century for the Trent Bridge club.

Courtney Walsh (1984–). Born in Kingston, Jamaica and educated at Excelsior High School, Courtney Walsh took 10 for 43 in an innings in school cricket in 1979. A year later, he was included in the Jamaica youth team against the England youth team on its tour of the Caribbean. On leaving school he joined the illustrious Melbourne Club and made his first-class debut in 1982. He ended the season as his side's leading bowler, having taken 6 for 95 against the champions, Barbados. The same year he represented Young West Indies on their tour of England, and in 1984 set a record for Jamaica by taking 30 wickets in the Shell Shield. Later that year he was selected for the full West Indies team to tour England and so was only available for six matches for Gloucestershire to whom he'd been recommended by Tom Graveney.

In 1985, his first full season with the County, he was responsible for moving Gloucestershire fourteen places up the Championship table as he finished with 85 wickets at 19.95. He returned home to be the leading wicket taker in the Shell Shield with 29 wickets at 15.89 each. On his return to England in 1986 he was the first bowler to 100 Championship wickets, reaching the landmark on 9 August, earlier than anyone since Lance Gibbs in 1971. He headed the first-class bowling averages with 118 wickets at 18.17 apiece including 9 for 72 against Somerset at Cheltenham, and returned five or more wickets in an innings in eleven other matches.

He has captained Gloucestershire and the West Indies and has at the time of writing 328 Test wickets. At County level he has been among the most penetrative bowlers on the circuit, claiming 763 victims at 20.38.

1990 team. Back row, left to right: G.A. Tedstone, E.T. Milburn, S.N. Barnes, K.B.S. Jarvis, G.D. Hodgson, N.M. Pritchard, R.C.J. Williams. Middle row: G.G.M. Wiltshire (coach), K.M. Curran, P.W. Romaines, I.P. Butcher, J.W. Lloyds, M.W. Alleyne, M.W. Pooley, M.C.J. Ball. Front row: A.W. Stovold, P. Bainbridge, A.J. Wright (captain), E.J. Barlow (manager), C.W.J. Athey, D.A. Graveney.

Though Courtney Walsh took 70 wickets in the Championship, including 8 for 58 against Northamptonshire and Kevin Curran 60 wickets and 1,261 runs with the bat, the County dropped four places to thirteenth. Bill Athey topped the batting averages with 1,384 runs at 53.23. There was an improvement in the Sunday League where the County finished eighth, but they finished bottom of their Benson and Hedges group and lost to Lancashire in the quarter-finals of the Nat West Trophy.

1992 team. Back row, left to right: M.G.N. Windows, R.C. Williams, T.H.C. Hancock, R.I. Dawson, A.M. Smith, M. Davies, R.C.J. Williams. Middle row: M.J. Gerrard, R.J. Scott, A.M. Babington, J.T.C. Vaughan, J.M. De la Pena, S.G. Hinks, R. Horrell, A.J. Hunt. Front row: M.C.J. Ball, M.W. Alleyne, R.C. Russell, C.W.J. Athey, A.J. Wright (captain), R.W. Rossiter (chairman), D.V. Lawrence, G.D. Hodgson, A.W. Stovold (coach).

After a carbon copy summer of 1990 the previous season, the return of Courtney Walsh, who topped the national bowling averages with 92 wickets at 15.96 runs apiece, the County moved up three places in the Championship to tenth. England wicket-keeper Jack Russell's batting improved so much that he topped the County averages with 904 runs at 47.57. The County had a poor Benson and Hedges Cup campaign, finishing bottom of their group of six, and were eliminated in the quarter-final of the Nat West Trophy by Essex. In the Sunday League the County both won and lost eight games to finish the season in eighth place.

Gloucestershire CCC 1989 Year Book cover, showing the main section of a sketch in colour especially drawn by Jack Russell at the 1988 Cheltenham Festival.

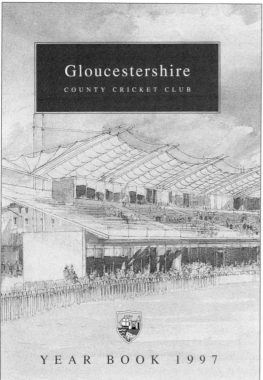

Gloucestershire CCC 1997 Year Book cover, showing an illustration of the new Jessop Stand.

1993 team. Back row, left to right: M.C.J. Ball, A.M. Smith, M. Davies, R.I. Dawson, T.H.C. Hancock, R.C.J. Williams. Middle row: B.H. Jenkins (scorer), R.C. Williams, S.G. Hinks, M.J. Gerrard, J.M. De la Pena, A.M. Babington, R.M. Wright, R. Horrell. Front row: G.D. Hodgson, M.W. Alleyne, A.W. Stovold (coach), P.G.M. August (secretary), A.J. Wright (captain), R.W. Rossiter (chairman), B.C. Broad, K.E. Cooper, R.J. Scott.

The County's disappointing season, in which they finished seventeenth in the Championship, ended with wins in two of their last three matches, enabling them to claw themselves above Durham. Courtney Walsh, who took 62 wickets at 23.64 each, put an end to the doubts about his future by accepting a new contract and the captaincy for the forthcoming season. Jack Russell, who had another good season with the bat, was appointed vice-captain and awarded a benefit in 1994. The County finished thirteenth in the Sunday League, lost to Derbyshire in the preliminary round of the Benson and Hedges Cup and were beaten by Yorkshire in the second round of the Nat West Trophy.

1994 team. Back row, left to right: R.C.J. Williams, K.P. Sheeraz, R.J. Cunliffe, D.R. Hewson, R.C. Williams, M.G.N. Windows. Middle row: B.H. Jenkins (scorer), M.C.J. Ball, V.J. Pike, A.M. Babington, S.G. Hinks, M.J. Cawdron, R.M. Wright, T.H.C. Hancock, R.I. Dawson, A.M. Smith, M. Davies. Front row: P.W. Romaines (assistant coach), A.J. Wright, B.C. Broad, A.W. Stovold (coach), R.W. Rossiter (chairman), P.G.M. August (secretary), G.D. Hodgson, M.W. Alleyne, K.E. Cooper.

Courtney Walsh had another magnificent season, taking 89 wickets at 17.24 each as the County moved up to twelfth in the Championship. He would have easily reached the 100 wicket mark but for a car crash, and then having to fly home to sort out his new national duties as West Indies captain.

However, there was disappointment in the one-day game as the County finished bottom of the Sunday League with just four wins, lost to Derbyshire in the first round of the Nat West Trophy and were beaten by Kent in the second round of the Benson and Hedges Cup after getting a bye in the first round.

Mark Alleyne (1986–). A product of the Haringey Cricket School, Mark Alleyne was just eighteen years old, the youngest player in the County's history to make a century, when he hit an unbeaten 116 against Sussex at Bristol in only his eighth first-class innings. Over the next few seasons he began to show a great maturity in his batting, and in 1990 finished third in the county averages with 763 runs at 44.88. Included in that total was the highest score of his career, a superb 256 against Northamptonshire. In 1991 he topped the 1,000 run mark, scoring 1,121 runs in all matches at an average of 32.02. He repeated the feat the following season, without making a century.

Appointed County captain in 1997, he didn't let the pressures affect his performances on the field, where he scored 1,059 runs at 40.73 and captured 44 wickets at 26.09 including a career best 6 for 64. Now ending his thirteenth season with the County, he has scored 10,239 runs and taken 254 wickets.

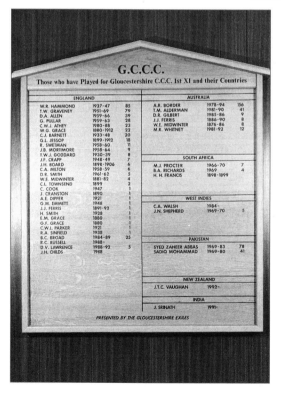

G.C.C.

Those who have Played for Gloucestershire C.C.C. 1st XI and their Countries

ENGLAND			AUSTRALIA		
W.R. HAMMOND	1927-47	85	A.R. BORDER	1978-94	156
T.W. GRAVENEY	1951-69	79	T.M. ALDERMAN	1981-90	41
D.A. ALLEN	1959-66	39	D.R. GILBERT	1985-86	9
G. PULLAR	1959-63	28	J.J. FERRIS	1886-90	8
C.W.J. ATHEY	1980-88	23	W.E. MIDWINTER	1876-86	8
W.G. GRACE	1880-1912	22	M.R. WHITNEY	1981-92	12
C.J. BARNETT	1933-48	20			
G.L. JESSOP	1899-1912	18			
R. SMETHAM	1958-60	11			
J.B. MORTIMORE	1958-64	9			
T.W.J. GODDARD	1930-39	8	SOUTH AFRICA		
J.F. CRAPP	1948-49	7			
J.H. BOARD	1898-1906	6	M.J. PROCTER	1966-70	7
C.A. MILTON	1958-59	6	B.A. RICHARDS	1969	4
D.R. SMITH	1961-62	5	H. H. FRANCIS	1898-1899	
W.E. MIDWINTER	1881-82	4			
C.L. TOWNSEND	1899	2			
C. COOK	1947	1			
J. CRANSTON	1890	1	WEST INDIES		
A.E. DIPPER	1921	1			
G.M. EMMETT	1948	1	C.A. WALSH	1984-	
J.J. FERRIS	1891-92	1	J.N. SHEPHERD	1969-70	5
H. SMITH	1928	1			
E.M. GRACE	1880	1			
G.F. GRACE	1880	1			
C.W.L. PARKER	1921	1			
R.A. SINFIELD	1938	1			
B.C. BROAD	1984-89	25	PAKISTAN		
R.C. RUSSELL	1988-		SYED ZAHEER ABBAS	1969-83	78
D.V. LAWRENCE	1988-92	5	SADIQ MOHAMMAD	1969-80	41
J.H. CHILDS	1988				
			NEW ZEALAND		
			J.T.C. VAUGHAN	1992-	
			INDIA		
			J. SRINATH	1991-	

PRESENTED BY THE GLOUCESTERSHIRE EXILES

Board showing those Gloucestershire players who have gained international recognition while with the County by playing Test match cricket.

Board showing Gloucestershire County Cricket Club Presidents from 1871 to present day.

GLOUCESTERSHIRE COUNTY CRICKET CLUB
PRESIDENTS

THE 8th DUKE of BEAUFORT, K.G., P.C., M.F.H.	1871-1899
THE 9th DUKE of BEAUFORT, M.F.H.	1900-1914
EARL BEAUCHAMP, K.G.	1919-1920
COL. SIR PERCIVAL MARLING, V.C., C.B.	1921-1922
R. E. BUSH, D.L., J.D.	1923-1924
LT. COL. J. N. HORLICK, M.C., M.P.	1925-1926
THE 10th DUKE of BEAUFORT, K.G., P.C., G.C.V.O., M.F.H.	1927-1928
	1936-1937
	1946-1971
LORD SHERBORNE, D.S.O., D.L., J.P.	1929-1930
SIR FOSTER G. ROBINSON,	1931-1932
SIR WALTER PRESTON, M.P.	1933-1934
F. O. WILLS, J.P.	1935
SIR STANLEY TUBBS, BART., J.P., M.P.	1938-1939
J. E. C. CLARKE, O.B.E., D.L.	1972-1973
R. F. P. HOLLOWAY,	1974-1975
M. R. MOORE, M.B.E.	1976-1977
B. O. ALLEN,	1978-1979
T. L. ROBINSON, T.D.	1980-1983
D. B. EVANS,	1983
J. K. R. GRAVENEY,	1984-1985
G. W. PARKER, O.B.E., T.D.	1986-1987
R. J. BERKELEY,	1988-1990
F. J. TWISELTON,	1990-1992
D. N. PERRY,	1992-1995
J. A. HORNE, J.P.	1995-

GLOUCESTERSHIRE COUNTY CRICKET CLUB

CHAIRMEN		TREASURERS		SECRETARIES	
1891-1914	H.W. Beloe	1870-71	H.M. Grace	1870-72	W.G. Grace
1919-22	R.E. Bush	1873-1905	W.H. Harford	1873-1909	E.M. Grace
1923-24	W.L. Olive J.P.	1906-14	H.W.L. Harford	1910-12	G.L. Jessop
1925-26	H. Walker D.L.J.P.	1920-35	A.J. Gardner	1913-14	C.O.H. Sewell
1927-35	A.J. Gardner	1936-39	A.J. Gardner & C.P. Lister	1919-21	W.T. Pearce
1936-56	F.O. Wills J.P.	1946-54	W.R. Giles	1922-35	W.G. Tunnicliffe
1957-62	Sir E. Lister D.L.	1955-56	C.H.G. Thomas M.C.	1936-41	Major H.A. Henson
1963-69	J.E.C. Clarke	1957-62	A.H.M. Derrick	1942-44	F.O. Wills J.P.
1970-72	M. Jarrett M.B.E.	1963-73	H.R.S. Bishop	1945-55	Lt.Col. H.A. Henson
1973-75	F.J. Twiselton	1974-81	R.W. Rossiter	1956-62	C.H.G. Thomas M.C.
1976-81	J.K.R. Graveney	1982	A.J. Vaughan	1963-66	R.J.G. McCrudden
1982-89	D.N. Perry T.D.	1984-85	A.J. Holmes	1967-76	G.W. Parker O.B.E.
1990-96	R.W. Rossiter	1986-	N.P. Walters	1976-82	A.S. Brown
1996-	J.C. Higeon			1982-86	D.G. Collier
				1986-	P.G.M. August

CAPTAINS			
1870	E.M. Grace	1968-76	A.S. Brown
1871-98	W.G. Grace	1977-81	M.J. Procter
1899	W.G. Grace & W. Troup	1982-88	D.A. Graveney
1900-12	G.L. Jessop	1989	C.W.J. Athey
1913-14	C.O.H. Sewell	1990-93	A.J. Wright
1919-21	Sir F.G. Robinson	1993-94	C.A. Walsh
1922-23	P.F.C. Williams	1995	R.C. Russell
1924-26	D.C. Robinson	1996-	C.A. Walsh
1927-35	W.H. Rowlands		
1929-33	B.H. Lyon		
1935-36	D.A.C. Page		
1937-38	B.O. Allen		
1939-46	W.R. Hammond		
1947-50	B.O. Allen		
1951-52	Sir D.T.L. Bailey Bart. D.F.C.		
1953-54	J.F. Crapp		
1955-58	G.M. Emmett		
1959-60	T.W. Graveney		
1961-62	C.T.M. Pugh		
1963	J.K.R. Graveney		
1964-66	J.B. Mortimore		
1967	C.A. Milton		

PRESENTED BY RAY PARSONS

Board showing the officials of Gloucestershire County Cricket Club – that is, the chairmen, treasurers, secretaries and captains.

1995 team. Back row, left to right: D.R. Hewson. R.J. Cunliffe, R.C.J. Williams, D.J.P. Boden, M.J. Cawdron, R.C. Williams. Middle row: K.P. Sheeraz, V.J. Pike, A.M. Smith, R.I. Dawson, M.C.J. Ball, T.H.C. Hancock, M. Davies, M.G.N. Windows, B.H. Jenkins (scorer). Front row: P.W. Romaines (assistant coach), A.J. Wright, A.W. Stovold (coach), R.C. Russell (captain), R.W. Rossiter (chairman), M.W. Alleyne, M.A. Lynch, G.D. Hodgson, K.E. Cooper.

With Courtney Walsh unavailable because of the West Indies tour of England, the County appointed Jack Russell as captain and he responded by leading them to sixth in the Championship, their best position since 1986. Walsh's replacement, Indian Test bowler Javagal Srinath, had a splendid season taking 87 wickets at 19.09 each. Andrew Symonds topped the County's batting averages with 1,346 runs at 56.08 including a magnificent unbeaten 254 against Glamorgan at Abergavenny. His innings contained a record 16 sixes and another four in his second knock gave him a record 20 sixes for the match. The County finished fifteenth in the Sunday League and reached the quarter-finals of both the Benson and Hedges Cup and Nat West Trophy, where they lost to Somerset and Northamptonshire respectively.

1996 team. Back row, left to right: D.R. Hewson, R.J. Cunliffe, K.P. Sheeraz, M.C.J. Ball, R.I. Dawson, T.H.C. Hancock, R.C.J. Williams. Middle row: M.A. Lynch, A.M. Smith, R.P. Davis, J. Whitby-Coles, M.J. Cawdron, A. Symonds, D.J.P. Boden, J. Lewis, K.E. Cooper, K.T. Gerrish (scorer). Front row: P.W. Romaines (assistant coach), M.W. Alleyne, R.C. Russell, J.C. Higson (chairman), A.J. Wright, A.W. Stovold (coach).

The County's disappointing season in which they finished thirteenth in the Championship ended rather more happily with wins in two of their last three matches against Northamptonshire and title-chasing Kent, the latter victims of Courtney Walsh, who had yet another productive season. Though he missed three matches, the West Indian's 85 Championship wickets were the biggest haul in the country and his strike rate of a wicket every six overs was outstanding. No-one made 1,000 runs in the Championship, although the County's other linchpin, Jack Russell, once again batted very valuably. The County were sixteenth in the Sunday League, lost to Somerset in the second round of the Nat West Trophy and were defeated by Lancashire in the quarter-final of the Benson and Hedges Cup.

1997 team. Back row, left to right: R.C.J. Williams, J. Lewis, R.F. Davis, M.J. Cawdron, N.J. Trainor, R.J. Cunliffe, M.G.N. Windows. Middle row: B.H. Jenkins (2nd XI scorer), M.C.J. Ball, D.R. Hewson, C.M.W. Read, K.P. Sheeraz, T.H.C. Hancock, R.I. Dawson, M.A. Lynch, S. Young, K.T. Gerrish (1st XI scorer). Front row: R.C. Russell, A.J. Wright, M.W. Alleyne (captain), D.V. Lawrence, A.W. Stovold (director of coaching), A.M. Smith.

Under the captaincy of Mark Alleyne, the County ended the season in seventh place in the Championship, with Jack Russell the leading batsman with 1,049 runs at 45.60. Remarkably this summer also saw both Alleyne and Russell pass the 10,000 run mark for the County. Shaun Young hit a fine 237 against Derbyshire at Cheltenham while the pick of the bowling was Mike Smith, whose 83 wickets at 16.56 each led to him being picked by England. The County finished eleventh in the Sunday League and disappointed in both the Benson and Hedges Cup and Nat West Trophy competitions.

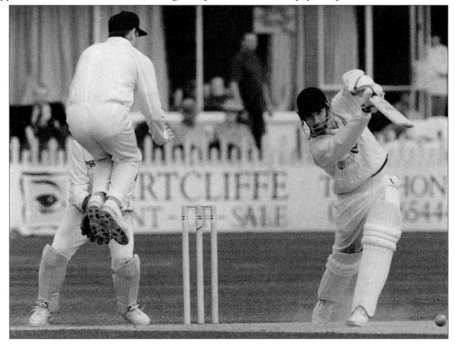

Mike Smith, Gloucestershire's latest Test debutant, renowned for his left-arm medium-fast bowling, produces a classical off-drive!

CHAPTER FIVE

COUNTY GROUNDS

Apart from the County Ground situated in Ashley Down, Gloucestershire have played on three other grounds in Bristol, Durdham Down, Clifton College and Greenbank. The only first-class match to be played at Durdham Down was against Surrey on 2, 3 and 4 June 1870. The first first-class match to be played at Clifton College was against Nottinghamshire on 3, 4 and 5 August 1871 and the last against All India on 6, 8 and 9 August 1932. Greenbank was owned by H.J. Packer (Chocolate Manufacturers) and known as 'Packer's Ground'. The first first-class match to be played there was against Sussex on 13 and 15 May 1922 and the last against Derbyshire on 28, 30 and 31 July 1928.

The present County Ground was laid out to W.G. Grace's specifications and the first game played there was against Lancashire on 1 and 2 July 1889.

The County have used three grounds in the town of Cheltenham and have staged a cricket festival at the College Ground since 1872, when Surrey were the opponents on 18 and 19 July. The County also used the East Gloucestershire Ground which was known as Charlton Park. It was first used by Gloucestershire against Nottinghamshire on 14, 15 and 16 June 1888 and last against Philadelphians on 15 and 16 June 1903. These were the only first-class matches played on the ground. The County also used the Victoria Ground in the town, first playing against Glamorgan on 27, 28 and 29 June 1923. They did not play again on the ground after the summer of 1937 until May 1986, when the Indians were the visitors.

Gloucestershire have played on three grounds in Gloucester, the first being the Spa Ground, which is now used by Gloucester City Cricket Club. The County's first match was against Yorkshire on 12, 13 and 14 July 1883 and the last against Leicestershire on 30, 31 May and 1 June 1923. The County then moved to the Wagon Works and played their first game against Lancashire on 2, 3 and 4 June 1923. The King's School in Gloucester is now used by the County.

Each season Gloucestershire travel to the Cotswold village of Moreton-in-Marsh to play a limited over match. The first visit was made in 1884 when a first-class match was staged with Yorkshire. The County also played at Batsford Road in 1886–8 and again in 1914, but it wasn't until the introduction of one-day cricket that the County returned. The first limited overs match at Moreton-in-Marsh was a Benson and Hedges Cup tie with Hampshire in 1972. Since then one match has been staged each season, usually in late August.

The County have also played a number of games on other grounds. On 28, 29 and 30 August 1879 the County played Surrey at Cirencester, the only first-class game to be staged at the ground. Lydney was first used by the County on 24, 26 and 27 August 1963 when the opponents were again Surrey and the last time six years later, when Sussex were the visitors. Stroud was first used on 9, 11 and 12 June 1956 when Gloucestershire's opponents were Nottinghamshire and the last against Glamorgan on

29, 30 and 31 May 1963, when the ground was lost because of industrial expansion. The ground at Swindon, which is located at the rear of Swindon Town Football Club, was first used by Gloucestershire in 1970 when a John Player Sunday League match was staged with Sussex. Not until fifteen years later did Gloucestershire return, this time when their Sunday opponents were again Sussex. A year later Essex were the visitors, and on this occasion Allan Border, the Australian captain, opened the new scorebox. Tewkesbury was used for two Sunday League games, against Yorkshire in 1972 and against Lancashire in 1973.

The Cheltenham College Cricket Ground photographed from the air.

The County Ground at Bristol is situated in Ashley Down on the northern outskirts of the city, the surrounding roads bearing the names of other first-class and minor counties. The County's previous home was Clifton College. The present ground was first used in 1889 against Lancashire and was laid out to W.G. Grace's specifications. In 1916 it was sold to the Fry's Chocolate Company to get the club out of debt and became known as the Fry's Ground. By 1932 the club was strong enough to buy back the ground after forming Gloucestershire County Cricket Club Limited. It is a ground with much character and the entrance to it on Nevil Road is through the Grace gates. The pavilion was built during the 1880s but other additions have been made in recent years. The Jessop Tavern was built in 1958 and the scoreboard in 1971. The mound stand was built during the 1960s, and the Grace Room and Hammond Room now form the restaurant at the Pavilion End.

Much has happened at Ashley Down: the remarkable tie with the Australian tourists in 1930, their revenge in that invincible tour of 1948 when they settled for 774 for 7, and Tom Goddard's 17 for 106 in one day against Kent in 1939.

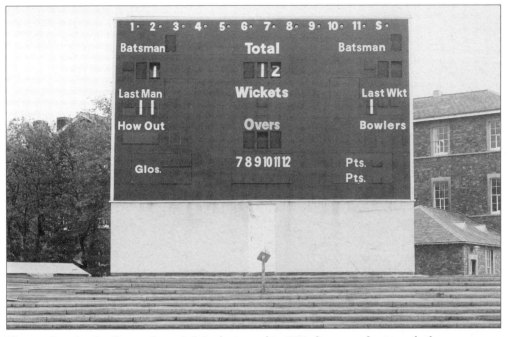

The scoreboard at the County Ground, Bristol, pictured in 1976, five years after it was built.

The Grace Room at the County Ground, Bristol is wood-panelled and rich in pictures. The famous hand of W.G. is preserved in casting, the face peers from table 171737 and the instantly recognisable figure stands nonchalantly between cricket ball ink-wells behind the pen-holder on the silver writing stand.

The Jessop Tavern, which also houses the press box, was built in 1958 and is placed appropriately at cover point. For Gilbert Jessop was a superlative fielder to which must be added fast bowling and, above all, fast batting!

Pictured under construction, the Hammond Room was built in 1977. Most visitors to the County Ground, I am sure, assume it refers to Walter. But in fact it is in memory of Cyril, one of the promotion chiefs so necessary nowadays. Along with the Grace Room, it forms the restaurant at the Pavilion End.

Net practice at the County Ground, Bristol.

The final match of the 1977 season saw Gloucestershire entertaining Hampshire at Bristol. The County were favourites for the Championship title, lying four points ahead of Middlesex and Kent. Gloucestershire scored 223 with Mike Procter making 115, and Hampshire replied with 229 with the South African taking 6 for 68. After Gloucestershire had scored 276 in their second innings, Hampshire needed 271 to win in 275 minutes. Unfortunately the visitors won by 6 wickets with eighty minutes to spare.

The Gloucestershire supporters waited for news, but with Middlesex and Kent winning the County had to settle for third position.

A section of the large crowd at the County Ground, Bristol for the match between Gloucestershire and Middlesex in 1947.

The first ground in Gloucester used by the County was the Spa Ground, between 1883 and 1921. The move to Tuffley Avenue came in 1923 when the first visitors were Lancashire. Since then the ground has had various names: first it was known as the Gloucestershire Railway Carriage and Wagon Company Ground until 1962; it was then taken over by the Gloucester Engineering Sports Club and then shortly afterwards the Babcocks and Wilcox Sports Club. Today it is known as the Winget Sports Ground.

Originally the ground was 33 acres and was bought by the railway carriage company in 1917 for £4,005. In 1973 20 acres were sold off for £525,000, the remaining acres forming the ground. The connection of railways with the Gloucester Ground is still quite prominent; the pavilion which serves the bowling green adjacent to the cricket pavilion is an old railway carriage. Around this time there might have been a housing estate on the field but the city council saved it from so inglorious a fate. The buildings are few – the pavilion completed in 1979 and the scoreboard which is something of a museum piece, for it came from Bristol's Ashley Down Ground. Ten plane trees line the pavilion boundary, while the old clubhouse was a hospital in the last war, having appropriately been built as a First World War hospital and brought here.

The ground has seen its fair share of records, including 317 from Walter Hammond against Nottinghamshire in 1936, his highest score in England, and at the Spa Ground in 1907 Northamptonshire were bowled out for only 12 runs.

The best crowd at the Gloucester ground was 9,000 in August 1959 for the match against Surrey.

Though crowds at the County Ground at Bristol are usually around 5–6,000 for popular matches, the best crowds were around 15,000 for the visits of the Australians in 1930 and 1948.

Gloucestershire have staged a cricket festival at the College Ground, Cheltenham since 1872. This used to take place in August after the college term had ended, but in recent years the festival has been held in July. The first match was against Surrey in July 1872 and the County have visited two other grounds in the town since, the East Gloucestershire Ground from 1888 until 1903 and the Victoria Ground from 1923 to 1937. In May 1986 the match against the Indians was played at Cheltenham Cricket Club because the College Ground was being used. Today the County play three Championship and two limited-over matches at the ground, and all are well supported.

The main permanent building on the ground used by the County is the gymnasium. It is used as a pavilion and stands on the Thirlestaine Road side of the ground. The College Chapel which overlooks the ground was built in 1893 and is probably the most significant feature of the College Ground.

The ground has seen many achievements over the years including 318 not out from W.G. Grace against Yorkshire in 1876. In 1896 Gloucestershire collapsed to 17 all out against the Australians. Cheltenham-born Gilbert Jessop hit 51 in eighteen minutes against Yorkshire in 1895 and Walter Hammond, who in his first match on the ground in 1928, scored 139 and 143 and took ten catches against Surrey. The County's overseas players must also have some fond memories of Cheltenham, for in 1979 Mike Procter had a hat-trick of lbws and Zaheer Abbas two years earlier scored 205 and 108 (both not out) in the match against Sussex.

Bert Avery in front of the portable scoreboard at Cheltenham. When Fred Dudderidge retired as Gloucestershire's scorer in 1971, Bert Avery achieved his ambition to enter professional sport at the age of fifty-five. From being an amateur player in local club cricket followed by club umpiring and scoring, he came up through the Bristol and District Cricket Association before accepting a vacancy for a scorer with the Gloucestershire second XI. When the vacancy for first team scorer occurred Bert had a problem, for he still worked with Shell-Mex, but in respect of his long service they generously gave him early retirement. Now, after twenty years as the County's scorer, he is the Museum Curator at the County Ground in Bristol.

APPENDICES

INNINGS TOTALS

Highest by the County

653–3 dec. *vs* Glamorgan at Bristol in 1928
643–5 dec. *vs* Nottinghamshire at Bristol in 1946
636 *vs* Nottinghamshire at Trent Bridge in 1904
634 *vs* Nottinghamshire at Bristol in 1898
625–6 dec. *vs* Worcestershire at Dudley in 1934

Highest Against the County

774–7 dec. by Australia at Bristol in 1948
607–6 dec. by Kent at Cheltenham in 1910
607 by Nottinghamshire at Bristol in 1899
594–6 dec. by Hampshire at Southampton in 1911
579 by Surrey at Bristol in 1901

Lowest by the County

17 *vs* Australia at Cheltenham in 1896
22 *vs* Somerset at Bristol in 1920
25 *vs* Somerset at Cheltenham in 1891
31 *vs* Kent at Tonbridge in 1903
31 *vs* Middlesex at Bristol in 1924

Lowest Against the County

12 by Northamptonshire at Gloucester in 1907
25 by Somerset at Bristol in 1947
31 by Somerset at Bristol in 1931
35 by Worcestershire at Cheltenham in 1928
35 by Yorkshire at Bristol in 1959

PARTNERSHIPS

County best for each wicket

1st	395	D.M. Young & R.B. Nicholls *vs* Oxford Univ. at Oxford 1962
2nd	256	C.T.M. Pugh & T.W. Graveney *vs* Derbyshire at Chesterfield 1960
3rd	336	W.R. Hammond & B.H. Lyon *vs* Leicestershire at Leicester 1933
4th	321	W.R. Hammond & W.L. Neale *vs* Leicestershire at Gloucester 1937
5th	261	W.G. Grace & W.O. Mobberly *vs* Yorkshire at Cheltenham 1876
6th	320	J.H. Board & G.L. Jessop *vs* Sussex at Hove 1903
7th	248	W.G. Grace & E.L. Thomas *vs* Sussex at Hove 1896
8th	239	W.R. Hammond & A.E. Wilson *vs* Lancashire at Bristol 1938
9th	193	W.G. Grace & S.A.P. Kitcat *vs* Sussex at Bristol 1896
10th	131	W.R. Gouldsworthy & J.G. Bessant *vs* Somerset at Bristol 1923

INDIVIDUAL BATTING

Over 10,000 runs in Gloucestershire career

		Inns	N.Os	Runs	H.Sc	Average	100s
W.R. Hammond	1920–51	664	74	33,664	317	57.05	113
C.A. Milton	1948–74	1,017	119	30,218	170	33.65	52
A.E. Dipper	1908–32	860	68	27,948	252*	35.28	53
R.B. Nicholls	1951–75	954	52	23,606	217	26.17	18
D.M. Young	1949–64	777	35	23,400	198	31.53	40
W.G. Grace	1870–99	612	49	22,808	318*	40.51	50
G.M. Emmett	1936–59	770	44	22,806	188	31.41	34
J.F. Crapp	1936–56	708	73	22,195	175	34.95	36
C.J. Barnett	1927–48	700	38	21,222	232	32.05	38
T.W. Graveney	1948–60	506	48	19,705	222	43.02	50
G.L. Jessop	1894–1914	605	23	18,936	286	32.53	36
A.W. Stovold	1973–90	617	35	17,460	212*	30.00	20
Zaheer Abbas	1972–85	360	37	16,083	230*	49.79	49
R.A. Sinfield	1924–39	684	83	15,561	209*	25.89	16
J.B. Mortimore	1950–75	928	114	14,918	149	18.32	4
W.L. Neale	1923–48	700	79	14,751	145*	23.75	14
M.J. Procter	1965–81	437	38	14,441	203	36.19	32
H. Smith	1912–35	645	55	13,334	149	22.60	10
B.O. Allen	1932–51	471	20	13,265	220	29.41	14
J.H. Board	1891–1914	755	74	13,092	214	19.22	8
A.J. Wright	1982–97	484	38	13,055	193	29.70	18
A.S. Brown	1953–76	797	98	12,684	116	18.14	3
P. Bainbridge	1977–90	420	60	12,281	169	34.11	22
S. Mohammed	1972–82	346	19	12,012	203	36.73	25
C.W.J. Athey	1984–92	303	37	11,383	181	42.63	28
D.R. Shepherd	1963–79	476	41	10,679	153	24.54	12
A.E. Wilson	1936–55	486	73	10,534	188	25.50	7
T. Langdon	1900–14	513	14	10,621	156	21.28	6
H. Wrathall	1894–1907	465	18	10,289	176	23.01	8
M.W. Alleyne	1986–97	359	37	10,239	256	31.79	13
R.C. Russell	1981–97	416	93	10,137	120	31.38	4

Most runs in a season

Runs	Average	Name	Season
2,860	69.75	W.R. Hammond	1933
2,637	71.27	W.R. Hammond	1927
2,583	78.27	W.R. Hammond	1928
2,571	65.92	W.R. Hammond	1937
2,554	75.11	Zaheer Abbas	1976
2,365	55.00	A.E. Dipper	1928
2,282	45.64	C.J. Barnett	1934
2,269	84.03	W.R. Hammond	1938
2,246	49.91	A.E. Dipper	1927

2,218	47.19	A.E. Dipper	1929
2,176	68.00	W.R. Hammond	1939
2,161	41.55	C.J. Barnett	1933
2,141	57.86	W.R. Hammond	1932
2,139	53.47	T.W. Graveney	1951
2,137	40.32	D.M. Green	1968
2,101	48.64	W.R. Hammond	1935
2,090	42.65	D.M. Young	1959
2,089	46.42	C.A. Milton	1967
2,081	22.41	W.R. Hammond	1934
2,072	37.00	A.E. Dipper	1926
2,059	36.76	R.B. Nicholls	1962

Double Centuries

318*	W.G. Grace *vs* Yorkshire at Cheltenham in 1876
317	W.R. Hammond *vs* Nottinghamshire at Gloucester in 1936
302*	W.R. Hammond *vs* Glamorgan at Bristol in 1934
302	W.R. Hammond *vs* Glamorgan at Newport in 1939
301	W.G. Grace *vs* Sussex at Bristol in 1896
290	W.R. Hammond *vs* Kent at Tunbridge Wells in 1934
288	W.G. Grace *vs* Sussex at Bristol in 1895
286	G.L. Jessop *vs* Sussex at Hove in 1903
271	W.R. Hammond *vs* Lancashire at Bristol in 1938
265*	W.R. Hammond *vs* Worcestershire at Dudley in 1934
264	W.R. Hammond *vs* Lancashire at Liverpool in 1932
264	W.R. Hammond *vs* West Indians at Bristol in 1933
257	W.G. Grace *vs* Kent at Gravesend in 1895
256	M.W. Alleyne *vs* Northants at Northampton in 1990
254	A. Symonds *vs* Glamorgan at Abergavenny in 1995
252*	A.E. Dipper *vs* Glamorgan at Cheltenham in 1923
252	W.R. Hammond *vs* Leicestershire at Leicester in 1935
250*	W.R. Hammond *vs* Lancashire at Old Trafford in 1925
247	A.E. Dipper *vs* Oxford University at Bristol in 1924
244	W.R. Hammond *vs* Essex at Chelmsford in 1928
243*	W.G. Grace *vs* Sussex at Hove in 1896
240	G.L. Jessop *vs* Sussex at Bristol in 1907
239	W.R. Hammond *vs* Glamorgan at Gloucester in 1933
238*	W.R. Hammond *vs* Warwickshire at Edgbaston in 1929
237	W.R. Hammond *vs* Derbyshire at Bristol in 1938
237	S. Young *vs* Derbyshire at Cheltenham in 1937
234	G.L. Jessop *vs* Somerset at Bristol in 1905
233	D.M. Green *vs* Sussex at Hove in 1968
232	C.J. Barnett *vs* Lancashire at Gloucester in 1937
231	W.R. Hammond *vs* Derbyshire at Cheltenham in 1933
230*	Zaheer Abbas *vs* Kent at Canterbury in 1976
228*	C.J. Barnett *vs* Leicestershire at Gloucester in 1947
224*	C.L. Townsend *vs* Essex at Clifton in 1899
223	C.C.R. Dacre *vs* Worcestershire at Worcester in 1930

222	T.W. Graveney *vs* Derbyshire at Chesterfield in 1954
220	B.O. Allen *vs* Hampshire at Bournemouth in 1947
218*	W.R. Hammond *vs* Glamorgan at Bristol in 1928
217	W.R. Hammond *vs* Nottinghamshire at Bristol in 1934
217	W.R. Hammond *vs* Leicestershire at Gloucester in 1937
217	R.B. Nicholls *vs* Oxford University at Oxford in 1962
216*	Zaheer Abbas *vs* Surrey at the Oval in 1976
215*	Zaheer Abbas *vs* Somerset at Bath in 1981
214	J.H. Board *vs* Somerset at Bristol in 1900
214	C.L. Townsend *vs* Worcestershire at Cheltenham in 1906
214	W.R. Hammond *vs* Somerset at Bristol in 1946
213	Zaheer Abbas *vs* Sussex at Hove in 1978
212*	A.W. Stovold *vs* Northants at Northampton in 1982
212	A.E. Dipper *vs* Worcestershire at Bristol in 1927
211*	W.R. Hammond *vs* Nottinghamshire at Bristol in 1946
211*	W.R. Hammond *vs* Oxford University at Oxford in 1930
211	T.W. Graveney *vs* Kent at Gillingham in 1953
210	G.W. Parker *vs* Kent at Dover in 1937
209*	R.A. Sinfield *vs* Glamorgan at Cardiff in 1935
207	W.R. Hammond *vs* Essex at Westcliff in 1939
206	G.L. Jessop *vs* Nottinghamshire at Trent Bridge 1904
206	W.R. Hammond *vs* Leicestershire at Leicester in 1933
206	D.N. Moore *vs* Oxford University at Oxford in 1930
205*	W.R. Hammond *vs* Surrey at the Oval in 1928
205*	Zaheer Abbas *vs* Sussex at Cheltenham in 1977
204*	C.J. Barnett *vs* Leicestershire at Leicester in 1936
203	M.J. Procter *vs* Essex at Gloucester in 1978
201	T.G. Matthews *vs* Surrey at Clifton in 1871
201	T.W. Graveney *vs* Sussex at Worthing in 1950
201	T.W. Graveney *vs* Oxford University at Oxford in 1951
201	T.W. Graveney *vs* Glamorgan at Newport in 1956

INDIVIDUAL BOWLING

Over 500 wickets in Gloucestershire career

		Runs	Wkts	Average
C.W.L. Parker	1905–35	61,600	3,169	19.43
T.W.J. Goddard	1922–52	56,062	2,862	19.58
E.G. Dennett	1903–26	41,412	2,083	19.88
C. Cook	1946–64	35,929	1,768	20.32
J.B. Mortimore	1950–75	38,946	1,695	22.71
W.G. Grace	1870–99	24,774	1,340	18.48
A.S. Brown	1953–76	31,159	1,223	25.47
R.A. Sinfield	1924–39	28,398	1,165	24.37
D.R. Smith	1956–70	27,449	1,159	23.68
F.G. Roberts	1887–1905	21,155	963	21.96

G.E.E. Lambert	1938–57	25,831	908	28.44
D.A. Allen	1953–72	19,515	882	22.12
M.J. Procter	1965–81	16,299	833	19.56
P.T. Mills	1902–29	20,708	823	25.16
D.A. Graveney	1972–90	23,688	815	29.06
C.A. Walsh	1984–97	15,555	763	20.38
C.L. Townsend	1893–1922	14,318	654	21.89
W.A. Woof	1878–1902	11,839	644	18.38
G.L. Jessop	1894–1914	13,866	620	22.36
H.J. Huggins	1901–21	16,953	584	29.02
B.D. Wells	1951–59	11,524	544	21.18
C.J. Scott	1938–54	16,766	531	31.57
W.R. Hammond	1920–51	14,801	504	29.36

Most Wickets in a Season

	Wickets	Average	Year
T.W. Goddard	222	16.80	1937
T.W. Goddard	222	16.37	1947
C.W.L. Parker	219	14.26	1931
C.W.L. Parker	206	14.75	1925
C.W.L. Parker	200	17.97	1926
T.W. Goddard	200	20.36	1935

Nine or More Wickets in an Innings

10–40	E. Dennett *vs* Essex at Bristol in 1906
10–66	J.K.R. Graveney *vs* Derbyshire at Chesterfield in 1949
10–79	C.W.L. Parker *vs* Somerset at Bristol in 1921
10–113	T.W. Goddard *vs* Worcestershire at Cheltenham in 1937
9–21	T.W. Goddard *vs* Cambridge University at Cheltenham in 1929
9–23	W.R. Hammond *vs* Worcestershire at Cheltenham in 1928
9–34	H.J. Huggins *vs* Sussex at Bristol in 1904
9–35	C.W.L. Parker *vs* Leicestershire at Cheltenham in 1920
9–36	C.W.L. Parker *vs* Yorkshire at Bristol in 1922
9–37	T.W. Goddard *vs* Leicestershire at Bristol in 1934
9–38	T.W. Goddard *vs* Kent at Bristol in 1939
9–41	T.W. Goddard *vs* Nottinghamshire at Bristol in 1947
9–42	C. Cook *vs* Yorkshire at Bristol in 1947
9–44	C.W.L. Parker *vs* Essex at Gloucester in 1925
9–44	T.W. Goddard *vs* Somerset at Bristol in 1939
9–46	C.W.L. Parker *vs* Northants at Northampton in 1927
9–48	C.L. Townsend *vs* Middlesex at Lord's in 1898
9–55	W.G. Grace *vs* Nottinghamshire at Cheltenham in 1877
9–55	T.W. Goddard *vs* Worcestershire at Bristol in 1939
9–56	J.H. Childs *vs* Somerset at Bristol in 1981
9–61	T.W. Goddard *vs* Derbyshire at Bristol in 1949
9–63	E.G. Dennett *vs* Surrey at Bristol in 1913
9–72	C.A. Walsh *vs* Somerset at Bristol in 1986

9–82   T.W. Goddard *vs* Surrey at Cheltenham in 1946
9–87   C.W.L. Parker *vs* Derbyshire at Gloucester in 1922
9–103   C.W.L. Parker *vs* Somerset at Bristol in 1927
9–111   R.A. Sinfield *vs* Middlesex at Lord's in 1936
9–118   C.W.L. Parker *vs* Surrey at Gloucester in 1925
9–128   C.L. Townsend *vs* Warwickshire at Cheltenham in 1898

WICKET-KEEPING

Most Dismissals in an Innings

6 (3ct 3st)   H. Smith *vs* Sussex at Bristol in 1923
6 (6ct)   A.E. Wilson *vs* Hampshire at Portsmouth in 1953
6 (6ct)   B.J. Meyer *vs* Somerset at Taunton in 1962

Most Dismissals in a Match

10 (10ct)   A.E. Wilson *vs* Hampshire at Portsmouth in 1953

Most Dismissals in a Season

75 (52ct 23st)   J.H. Board 1895
70 (55ct 15st)   B.J. Meyer 1964

Most Career Dismissals

982 (678ct 304st)   J.H. Board 1891–1914

FIELDING

Most Catches in an Innings

7   A.S. Brown *vs* Nottinghamshire at Trent Bridge in 1966

Most Catches in a Match

10   W.R. Hammond *vs* Surrey at Cheltenham in 1928

Most Catches in a Season

78   W.R. Hammond in 1928

Most Catches in a Career

718   C.A. Milton   1948–74
551   W.R. Hammond   1920–51
485   A.S. Brown   1953–76

ACKNOWLEDGEMENTS

I would like to express my most sincere thanks to the following individuals and institutions who helped me in the compilation of this book.

Of great importance was Bert Avery (former scorer and now museum curator at Gloucestershire County Cricket Club), who kindly loaned me a wealth of photographic material for inclusion in the book and without which this publication would not have been possible. I would also like to take this opportunity of thanking Bert for his kind hospitality following my eventful journey to Bristol in November 1997!

Thanks also to Peter Stafford (former Bolton League Secretary and now on the Executive Committee of Lancashire County Cricket Club) for the loan of Gloucestershire County Cricket Club cigarette cards from his vast collection.

A small minority of photographs were from the *Lancashire Evening Post* and my own private collection.

BRITAIN IN OLD PHOTOGRAPHS

SUTTON'S PHOTOGRAPHIC HISTORY OF TRANSPORT

To order any of these titles please telephone our distributor, Littlehampton Book Services on 01903 82880(
For a catalogue of these and our other titles please ring Regina Schinner on 01453 731114